LUIZ FELIPE SCOLARI

LUIZ FELIPE SCOLARI

THE MAN, THE MANAGER

José Carlos Freitas

dewi lewis media

LUIZ FELIPE SCOLARI
The Man, The Manager
by José Carlos Freitas

This edition first published in the UK in 2008 by
Dewi Lewis Media Ltd
8, Broomfield Road
Heaton Moor
Stockport SK4 4ND
www.dewilewismedia.com

Original publication in Portugal in July 2008 by Prime Books

> Editors: Dewi Lewis & Caroline Warhurst

> Portuguese football advisor: Adam Gumbley

> Translation: Silvia Baptista

> Design and Artwork Production: Dewi Lewis Media Ltd

> Print and binding: Gutenberg Press, Malta

ISBN: 978-1-905928-05-7

10   9   8   7   6   5   4   3   2   1

FOREWORD

On 11 June 2008 Chelsea announced the appointment of Luiz
Felipe Scolari as their new manager, with effect from July 1.

It was the end of months of speculation which had begun even
before Avram Grant's tenure as Chelsea boss had finally ended
on May 24. Despite having taken Chelsea to their first ever
Champions League Final, to the Carling Cup Final and to runners
up position in the Premier League, Grant's season was deemed a
failure – that his Chelsea team had twice lost out to Alex
Ferguson's Manchester United probably didn't help. It seemed
that coming second was not an option. Chelsea had greater
ambitions.

Following José Mourinho was never going to be an easy task
and Grant struggled to win the support of the fans. Even after
Mourinho's departure in September 2007, they continued to
chant Mourinho's name, unfurling banners at Stamford Bridge
that read 'Mourinho: The Special One'. As the months passed,
the fans became more forgiving and Grant began to garner
respect for his composure and resilience in the face of continued
pressure – and because he seemed to be a very decent human
being. Yet there were always lingering doubts.

The Press were equally dismissive. Never the natural
communicator that Mourinho had been, Grant's press conference
performances were increasingly ridiculed as the season
progressed. In early April, following a Chelsea win against
Everton, his responses were strangely monosyllabic. The press
derided him mercilessly:

«Avram GRANT turned into Avram GRUNT as he
completely lost the plot last night.» – *The Sun*

«A typical Grant press call sounds like a Book of Condolence being read aloud by a sedated undertaker who secretly hated the deceased. The Chelsea manager bristles at the portrayal of him as dour and taciturn, and those who know the man profess to like him. But although obviously bright, he has what a mother would describe as 'an unfortunate way about him'.» – *The Daily Mail.*

«With his sunken eyes and dour demeanour, the caricature of Grant as the accidental Chelsea manager is one which has haunted him.» – *The Sun.*

Many commentators felt that Chelsea FC weren't much more supportive either. There were continual reports of player unrest and the attitude of senior management also appeared ambiguous:

«Avram has got on with the job quietly and efficiently,» Chief Executive, Peter Kenyon commented at one point, with less than overwhelming enthusiasm.

Losing the Champions League Final to Manchester United was a crushing blow for Grant. It was clear how deeply disappointed he was by the cruel fate of the penalty shoot-out and it generated a sympathy at many levels. It was reported that the generous round of applause that Grant received from the press, as he left his last post-match press call at Moscow's Luzhniki stadium, was even louder than the one that a triumphant Alex Ferguson received minutes later. But it was all too little, too late.

And now it is the turn of Luiz Felipe Scolari.

Already known to English football fans as the man who turned down the England job back in April 2006, the realisation of the extent of press intrusion that went with the job was, at the time, enough reason for him to say no. Yet now he had decided to take on one of the highest profile jobs in English football.

He may not have the flamboyance of Mourinho, but he is a natural communicator, at ease not only with the press but also as a public speaker who has, for years, given talks at corporate and other events.

His reputation on the football pitch is immense. A World Cup winner with Brazil, he has managed 14 clubs in 5 different countries. The fluidity and style of his Portugal team over recent years suggests that he is well able to bring Stamford Bridge the attractive football that Roman Abramovich has so long dreamt of for his Chelsea team. Already though Scolari has added his own proviso: «…sometimes, it's impossible to play beautifully because the other team plays a different style.»

Chelsea defender, Ricardo Carvalho, who was a member of his Portuguese team has said: «He is a great manager and a big personality. He's the kind of guy that players respond to.»

Other players seem to agree and already there seems to be a warming to him, John Terry reportedly saying that they «now have a proper manager» and Frank Lampard confirming a new five year contract.

The fans are equally positive. The long shadow cast by José Mourinho may not have totally faded but once again it seems that Chelsea have a manager perfectly able to hold his own against the likes of Alex Ferguson and Arsène Wenger – a proven winner, a strong leader with a warrior spirit, and a man that the players and the fans admire and trust.

The Scolari era has begun!

Dewi Lewis

LUIZ FELIPE SCOLARI

CONTENTS

After almost 30 years, I can finally dedicate my work to those dearest to me: my parents, Mário and Laura, my brother Luís and my sister Céu, my children, Joao and Diogo, my wife, Dulce. I kiss you all and thank you for your patience.

This book wouldn't have been possible without the effort, commitment and invaluable help of Jaime Cancella de Abreu, my original Portuguese publisher, who I thank for trusting in me from our first meeting – at a lunch with my friend José Manuel Freitas.

José Carlos Freitas

I decided to write this book in September 2007, immediately after the incident between Scolari and the Serbian player Dragutinovic (Scolari had been accused of striking the player during a pitch-side altercation and the matter had become a matter for a disciplinary review at FIFA). I wanted to write something about the role that Scolari had played, managing and developing the Portuguese national team. It seemed at that time that his five years of hard work could be at risk, vanishing in a second because of this one ill-considered action, which although it was something to be condemned, was being used and abused by those who had always looked on Scolari with disdain.

In a free society such as ours everyone has the right to an opinion. I do not condemn, nor will I ever, people who criticise Scolari, whether or not I feel it is with or without good reason. What I truly don't understand is what seems to be an increasingly prevalent trend these days – that people will happily say all sorts of thing about a man to whom they have never personally spoken, a manager to whom they have never put a question, either at a press conference or in an individual one-to-one interview.

During the last 25 years, I've attended more than 130 games of the Portuguese national team, either as a journalist or as Press Officer for the Portuguese Football Federation, I've closely followed all the managers that have worked with the national team during that period and enjoyed meeting them but, for me, meeting Luiz Felipe Scolari has been the most pleasurable experience. For two simple reasons: he's always been professional, available, always making it very clear as to what was on or off the record – but also because the man behind the manager has proven to be much more captivating and interesting than the image that the media portrays of him.

Not surprisingly this book focuses on Scolari's period as the manager of the Portuguese national team, from his arrival in January 2003 until the end of Euro 2008 and his move to Chelsea FC. It's also my thoughts and my impressions of the man, thoughts that I felt obliged to share with everybody who loves football, and particuarly Portuguese football, and with those millions of people that have both suffered and rejoiced with Portugal's good and bad results. It is also about Luiz Felipe, the man behind Scolari – a man who's no saint but neither is he the devil that some people insist on presenting him as. He is a manager who has made mistakes but one who has also taken brave decisions and with Portugal he has led the team to levels of competition never previously experienced.

HIRING THE WORLD CHA
HELLO TO PORTU

João Rodrigues, a renowned lawyer from Lisbon, was a member of the Portuguese delegation at the World Cup draw, in 2002. A former president of the Portuguese Football Federation (FPF) and, at the time, a member of the FIFA disciplinary committee, Rodrigues had picked up whispers and rumours behind the scenes that Luiz Felipe Scolari had decided to leave the Brazilian national team, regardless of the results of the World Cup. Armed with this information, he and Gilberto Madaíl, the FPF president, took the decision to invite Luiz Felipe Scolari to dinner and, although nothing other than an informal conversation had been planned, Madaíl took the opportuinty to announce:

«One day you'll be the manager of Portugal.»

At that point, Scolari's response was formal and polite:

«I'd be honoured.»

Portugal had high expectations for the 2002 World Cup – expectations that they totally failed to live up to. Eliminated at the group stage – in the group that also included the United States and South Korea – they had only a single victory, against Poland. But even worse than the poor results were the innumerable stories that were circulating about the Portuguese team – stories of indiscipline as well as of bad planning and poor preparation. The manager at the time was António Oliveira, and at the end of the competition he was sacked.

Over the following months, during the process of searching for a new manager, Gilberto Madaíl came under enormous pressure. He was involved in secret talks with the manager

oaching the Egyptian team Al-Ahly at
African Champions League). All of this
it fell through, though the exact reason
I was told that FC Porto had voiced their
ne else told me that it was because some
ayers in the Portugal team didn't agree
nd that their word had been decisive.
(Following Scolari's move to Chelsea reports again surfaced that
Manuel José would take over the Portuguese national team but,
in the end, the Portuguese Football Federation hired former
Manchester United Assistant Coach, Carlos Queiroz).

João Rodrigues was having lunch with Miguel Ribeiro Telles
(President of Sporting Lisbon), to deal with issues surrounding a
case that was pending at FIFA against the player João Pinto, who
had hit the Argentinean referee during Portugal's World Cup
match against South Korea.

Telles turned to Rodrigues and asked him:

«Have you heard who's going to be the new manager?»

«I suppose he'll be foreign,» Rodrigues suggested.

But Telles surprised him by revealing a name: Manuel José.

After the poor results during the World Cup, Madaíl didn't
want to take any risks. The choice had to be unanimous,
something which was not going to be an easy task, particularly as
Manuel José was not a name on which there was general
agreement. Rodrigues, who has always been very close to
Madaíl, suggested that they consider Scolari.

«Are you insane?» was Madaíl's first and immediate reaction.
He was not alone in thinking that it was impossible for the
Federation to consider Scolari because its financial position was
not healthy enough for the salary he would require. Nevertheless,
Rodrigues persuaded Madaíl to pursue the idea and it wasn't long
before someone finally whispered to Scolari that there was

Portuguese interest. Luiz Felipe provided his home number for any future contact.

The first phone call was hilarious. Madaíl called, only to be greeted by someone with a thin, child-like voice who replied:

«Daddy's not at home.»

Madaíl was not fooled, however.

«Not at home?»

He paused a moment then continued,

«Mr. Scolari this is Gilberto Madaíl speaking, president of the FPF....»

The childish voice disappeared immediately:

«Mr. President, it's me, of course. I'm sorry but I had to talk like this because the French are harassing me big time.»

By 'the French' he meant the bosses at Paris Saint-Germain, who over the previous few weeks had almost convinced Scolari to move from Porto Alegre to Paris. However, when he heard that the FPF were considering him as a potential manager he had decided to wait to hear the Portuguese proposal. The same day that he and Madaíl spoke on the phone Scolari stalled Paris Saint-Germain further by asking for a little more time to consider their proposal.

Despite not knowing any of the real details of the Portuguese proposal, Scolari was intrigued and decided to discuss it with his wife, Dona Olga, who has always been a strong influence whenever he has to make an important career decision. Her advice was straightforward and to the point:

«Listen Felipe, I think you should take notice of Presidente Madaíl.»

And so he did.

The two of them met together in Guadalupe, near Seville in Spain. On his return to Lisbon, Madaíl talked with Rodrigues and explained to him that no matter how interesting Scolari was as a future manager there was no way that they could afford to hire him. His salary was just impossibly high for the FPF. But Rodrigues didn't give up and began to search out potential sponsors who might be able provide additional funding to solve the problem. In the end he succeeded with the decisive support of BPN Bank, who purchased Scolari's image rights, and Nike, the team's kit brand. Madaíl was able to close the deal with Scolari.

But the president still had another problem to solve, namely Manuel José. Luckily for Madaíl, he had never gone public about his discussions or talked about the pre-agreement that he had reached. In the end though the FPF had to pay compensation to Manuel José, based on the pre-agreement that they'd made, and the case was closed. The Portuguese Football Federation were finally off the hook.

On December 15th 2002 the Brazilian manager was formally and officially introduced as Manager of the Portuguese team. At the press conference he immediately stamped his own unique style on things, making it clear how he intended to move forward.

«I want discipline, honour and loyalty,» he said, adding, as if disclosing the criteria by which he would choose any future team, «I have to talk with the players a couple of times, get to know their personalities and how they behave as a group and figure out in what ways they can help the team.»

A month later, on 14 January 2003, Scolari began work. Now· 'crowned' the World Cup winning manager, he set the bar high:

«I cannot, on the one hand, say that my mindset is a winning one and, on the other, not expect to reach the Euro 2004 final.»

DEALING WITH THE PRESS
A RATHER GENTLE FIRST ENCOUNTER

Everybody knows that Scolari can give journalists a very hard time, particularly those that he doesn't know. During the period when he was negotiating with the FPF this was already a well-known characteristic of the man. He had form.

Whilst managing the Brazilian national team, and during the last stages of preparation for the World Cup 2002, a story had broken in the media saying that the Brazilian players had been given porn magazines. Whilst it was totally false it still caused quite a stir. As is usual with these things there always has to be a response and so the team's press officer was calmly writing a statement to release to the press. Scolari on the other hand was less calm. Deeply offended by the story, he stormed out of his hotel room and went down to the hotel lobby to face the reporter who had written the story. The result was an extremely powerful verbal assault on the ambushed journalist.

During the World Cup, another similar case arose. This time the contretemps was with a photographer who was hanging on the door of the team bus while furiously taking pictures of Scolari. Despite requests to stop the photographer continued snapping and Scolari himself snapped.

At the end of the 1990s, while working at Palmeiras, he had punched a reporter after a verbal dispute. Again it was motivated by a news report which had angered him. The journalist in question had written that Scolari had obstructed team supporters from watching the team while they were training. Once again it was a fabricated story and Scolari's response was vigorous.

Barriers between Scolari and journalists can take a long time to break down and in the real world there isn't always the opportunity. For that reason, the work of the journalist isn't always easy. When news of the negotiations between the FPF and Scolari became known he had his first glimpse of what it would be like dealing with the Portuguese press. At the time he was on holiday with his family in Rome. He found that he was being constantly followed wherever they went, tourist sites, parks, restaurants or just wandering the city streets. Even during a trip to the Vatican they were stalked, this time by a photographer who had disguised himself as a tourist to take pictures of him.

It wasn't long before Scolari understood that it was inevitable and that he could no longer proceed without saying at least a few words to the Portuguese press. He agreed to make a statement, and an improvised press conference was set up in one of the hotels. It was the first face-to-face with that group of reporters. In the end it was a fairly relaxed affair – almost just a normal conversation – no strong headlines, just the confirmation of what everybody already knew: that he was negotiating with Madaíl, that the FPF was studying the proposal he had made and that, in case of acceptance, he promised that he would do his best for the Portuguese team.

Scolari played it in a very placid and non-aggressive way and the result was that most journalists filed reports that suggested that Scolari was actually rather calm and quiet – a very taciturn manager.

A PROFESSIONAL APPROACH
AND A PLEASANT SURPRISE

For most people who have followed Portuguese football, the impression has always been that the so called 'big' clubs are far more professional and organised than the Portuguese Football Federation itself. My experience however has been rather different. Scolari's first professional contact with the Federation also made a very good impression on him, though at the time, because of his quiet nature, he didn't say anything about it.

Carlos Godinho, a key-man in the FPF's organisation and Technical Director for the Euro 2008 Portuguese squad, handed over a large number of files full of information that Scolari hadn't even known existed. They contained details of the fifty players that had played for the Portuguese team in the previous four years, a dozen videos of games that had taken place before and during the Korean World Cup, as well as videos of some other games during the period of Agostinho Oliveira's management, medical reports (always important to Scolari) and a lot more material. That day Scolari took home an enormous amount of homework as, at that time, he knew little about Portuguese football.

It was a kind of crash course for him. Something that he had to work through in the month prior to his arrival in post, and in his first month after being presented as the new manager. Scolari, Murtosa (Flávio 'Murtosa' Teixeira, Scolari's no. 2) and Darlan Schneider (His Fitness Coach) began to get a sense of what they were about to encounter on the pitch. For Darlan, however, there was the slight disadvantage that until then the Portuguese team had never had a full-time Fitness Manager. Once in Lisbon, one of Scolari's first decisions was, after discussion with Carlos Godinho, to order the necessary technical material to support his training programmes. The second one was to prepare a list of websites on which he could find information about Portuguese players who were playing abroad.

Scolari's priority was to determine the team sheet for a particular game with Italy, which was to be played in Genoa. He already knew how much pressure the former manager Agostinho Oliveira had been under. At a farewell party in his hometown of Porto Alegre, immediately before he moved to Lisbon, he said:

«I know I'll have problems with my first three team sheets although it's clear that after that everything will be okay.»

Maybe that's why he decided that for his first match he would select primarily from amongst those players that had played during the former manager's reign.

THE SOUL MATE
TOGETHER FOR MORE THAN 20 YEARS

After almost twenty five years of working together, Luiz Felipe Scolari and Flávio Teixeira (Murtosa) are to continue side by side – this time in what is seen as the most competitive and spectacular league in the world, the Premier League – managing Chelsea FC, the club of the Russian multi-billionaire Roman Abramovich.

Many are curious to know how they work together, how their personalities fit each other, what really are Teixeira's skills – who is that short and rather discreet man that Scolari has chosen to be his side kick.

It was in 1982 that Murtosa, as he's known by his friends and his family, started his management career in Esporte Clube Pelotas, having previously been the Fitness Manager at Grémio Atlético Farroupilha. Rather strangely, the President of Pelotas had also hired another manager, also just at the start of his career – Luiz Felipe Scolari. Murtosa knew almost nothing about him, and so the first few days of the relationship were unusual to say the least, and probably a little strained. No one really knew who was in charge – or of what – though Scolari was formally the 'lead' manager.

The atmosphere was far from pleasant and so Murtosa invited Scolari to lunch in an attempt to clear the air:

«We'll have to sort this out,» he said. «The president is just waiting for an excuse to interfere with our work. I know the players here better than you and I can help with decision making as long as you respect my work. If you're going to be lead manager then that is fine by me as long as we confirm that once and for all.»

Scolari, who was not used to someone being that upfront and honest, thanked Flávio for his comments and advice and together they managed to reach an agreement. As Flávio recalls, smiling, it was an agreement which allowed them to 'handle each other patiently'.

Born in Pelotas, Rio Grande do Sul, grandson of Portuguese emigrants from Murtosa, a village near the Portuguese coastal city of Aveiro, Flávio Teixeira has left Scolari only twice in his career. Once in 1997, to manage Juventude de Caxias, and in 2000, to manage Palmeiras, where Scolari had also worked before winning the Brazilian Cup and the Libertadores Cup.

For Portuguese supporters, Murtosa stepped into the public eye when he had to fill in for Scolari on the bench during the first three Euro 2008 qualifying games after Scolari was punished by UEFA with a touchline ban after punching Dragutinovic. He proved to be very successful with wins in Azerbaijan (2-0), Kazakhstan (2-1) and in Portugal, against Armenia (1-0).

That wasn't, however, the first time that he had filled Scolari's shoes. On 23 July 2001, in Colombia, Murtosa managed the Brazilian team in a match against Honduras, for the quarter-final of the America Cup (Copa América), where they lost 2-0. The curious thing though was that Murtosa shouldn't have been on the field managing the team – even though he was. Five days earlier, in a game against Paraguay, Scolari had been sent off after the first five minutes and Murtosa himself had also been banished at the end of the game for kicking the ball away. He, however, felt that it was an involuntary action, an impulse, and as a result he believed that the sentence was unduly harsh. The referee who sent off the two managers was the Argentinean Angel Sanchez, the same referee who was to send off João Pinto in the 2002 World Cup match against South Korea (João Pinto, in turn, retaliated by punching the referee and ended up being suspended for six months).

With both managers suspended, Brazil tried to fool the America Cup organisers. Scolari was someone whose face everybody knew, Murtosa's was not. And so it seemed worth trying a little subterfuge. Murtosa recalls the story with the grin of a little boy who has been caught out stealing cookies from the jar:

«It was very cold in Colombia and so I used a hood that covered part of my face. Then I took a doctor's bag and went and sat on the bench, next to the Fitness manager. I gave instructions onto the pitch without anyone noticing. But then at the end of the game I was caught out – unveiled by the TV coverage – and I was told to leave.»

«Brazil lost that game but our aim was to test out some players ready for the qualifying World Cup games. With Portugal it was different. We needed to win those three games and we did, with a great deal of effort from the players.»

During what was an important period for Portugal's aspirations, there was a lot of discussion about the personality differences between Scolari and Murtosa. The truth is they can be considered as two sides of the same coin, soul mates who understand and complement each other in the complex and competitive arena of football.

«Of course we have different personalities,» confirms Flávio Murtosa. «If we were the same we could not possibly get along this well. But that doesn't mean we agree on everything. Felipe has always listened to me and understood my opinions. He has always respected me as a coach, and has never expected me to act as a 'yes man'. Not that that is something I could ever be.»

Flávio Murtosa is a man who has always had an exemplary,

professional approach towards me and to most of the reporters who have followed his work and that of Scolari over the years. When one day I asked him how he could work with such a stubborn man as Scolari, Murtosa laughed and said:

«Felipe might seem to be a stubborn man but he listens to everybody's opinions and changes his own if he realises that he is wrong. He thinks for himself and he's nobody's fool.»

Luiz Felipe and Murtosa consider that they are 'like brothers'. They enjoy going out together for an early morning jog, or spending time together sitting around drinking tea as they used to back in their hometown. But, as they both say, in their free time they try to make sure that they «don't talk about football, although that's hard...»

Murtosa is a very competent man with a profound knowledge of football. For him there are no regrets about having given up his own career as a manager to follow Scolari all over the world:

«I'm working with a champion, a man with tremendous willpower, a winning mindset, someone capable of evolving. How can I complain?»

THE FIRST CONTROVERSY
VITOR BAÍA OUT

A few days before Scolari's first press conference at which he was due to announce the team sheet for his first match, he asked Carlos Godinho to take him to the hotel where FC Porto usually stay when they are in Lisbon. He wanted to talk with José Mourinho, who at the time was managing Porto – the team which provided most players for the Portuguese national side. He wanted to ask Mourinho's opinion about some of his players and Mourinho had agreed to a meeting. They spoke for quite a while, openly, trying to make sure that they understood each other's position and that everything was running smoothly.

A week later, when the team sheet was announced, the Porto goalkeeper Vitor Baía was excluded, despite having been a stalwart in the national team for a decade and having won a record 80 international caps. Half an hour later, Mourinho, during his usual press conference before FC Porto games, was the first to react to what he saw as a scandalous absence. He stated that whilst he fully respected Scolari's decisions:

«Baía is by far, and I repeat, by far, the best goalkeeper in Portugal.»

Scolari was appalled by the statement.

Even today there is still speculation as to why Baía was omitted from Scolari's first team selection. My theory is simple.

Just before Scolari arrived, Baía had not been available as an option for the former manager, Agostinho Oliveira. Against Tunisia (12 October 2002 in Lisbon, 1-1), Ricardo (Boavista) played in goal with Quim (Braga) on the bench; the next game, four days later, in Switzerland (Portugal won 3-2), the same two were selected but this time Quim was playing and Ricardo was on the bench; finally, against Scotland (November 20th 2002, 2-0 for Portugal), Quim was again playing and Nélson (Sporting Lisbon) was on the bench.

Baía was not included because when Agostinho Oliveira had intended to select him, there had been a disciplinary incident between the goalkeeper and José Mourinho which led to FC Porto officials 'blocking' the selection. This incident had led to Baía being on the bench initially and then to a disciplinary action that for a while removed him from any activity with the club.

For me, this solves the mystery. At the beginning Scolari only intended to call up those players who had been used by the former manager – and Baía was not amongst them. But once news of the criticism that Mourinho had raised at his press conference became known, Scolari felt that if he called up Baía for the next game – as I'm sure he had considered – then he would be giving in to outside pressure. And so for this reason, he was forced to make a point in a stronger way than he had originally intended.

«If I don't interfere in the club's work then I cannot possibly accept that they should interfere with mine,» Scolari told me later, more than once.

I have another theory on this subject that results from several conversations Scolari had with most of the players in his early months of work: some of them did actually complain about the goalkeeper.

One factor that Scolari took into consideration was Baía's past record with the Portuguese team, before the World Cup in South Korea and Japan. He soon realised that Baía hadn't played a single game during the qualifying stages and only became the number one choice during the finals themselves. During the conversations with the players, it appeared to Scolari that bringing Baía back could create some instability amongst his group of players. These were the reasons that brought an end to Baía's positon in the Portuguese team. And of course, Scolari had two good alternatives, Quim and Ricardo. Ultimately he was unwilling to risk upsetting the team spirit, disrupting things, just for the sake of one player. Not that Scolari intended to have only 'Yes men' in his squad – as people were to find out later – but at that point he could happily do without any instability.

Scolari and Baía only met once. Ricardo, the other goalkeeper, was also there. They bumped into each other on their way to an 'All Stars' game, a charity match that was being held in Switzerland. During the stopover in Frankfurt, Scolari, Carlos Godinho, Murtosa and Ricardo, who had travelled from Lisbon, met Vitor Baía and Paulo Ferreira, who had come from Porto. They ended up sitting in the same row on the plane for their onward flight and conversation was unavoidable. It was all very civilised, they talked about football but no one raised the issue of the Portuguese national team.

The first eleven players chosen by Scolari were Ricardo, Fernando Couto, Fernando Meira and Ricardo Costa; Sérgio Conceição, Tiago, Rui Costa and Nuno Valente; Figo, Pauleta and Simão. If we compare this team with the one that challenged for Euro 2008 we can see that only two players still remained: Ricardo and Simão. Scolari had quietly reorganised the team in his own mould during his five years in charge of the Portuguese team.

*I believe firmly
in astrology.
Since I was a kid,
the stars told me
I was a winner.*

THE DECO CONTROVERSY
WINNING CHOICE

Shortly after the Vitor Baía controversy, Scolari faced yet another one: this time with Deco. At the time he was playing for FC Porto, and had just gone through the naturalisation process to become a Portuguese citizen. Now he became an option for the manager to consider.

It's important to stress the point that Deco was not unknown to Scolari. On the contrary, he had already studied Deco as a player while he was manager of the Brazilian team, in particular at a Real Madrid-FC Porto match. However, his fondness and admiration for Deco and his respect for his football skills grew when Scolari came to Portugal.

In 2003, Deco was considered the best foreign player in the Portuguese championship. During the first press conference for the game against Brazil, the first match for which Scolari had called up Deco, the manager said:

«Deco is versatile, he is a fine striker of the ball and will be able to develop much more once he's got used to the squad.»

But the process wasn't easy. The Portuguese press had been talking about the possibility for months. When Deco missed an FC Porto training session to rush through the whole naturalisation process, everybody began to speculate that he might be called up to the Portuguese team sooner than had been expected, for the match against Italy. Nevertheless, Scolari, faithful to his principle of only talking about the players he intended to play, said:

«As far as that particular player is concerned I'll talk about him when he's ready to play.»

Asked about similar situations in the past in which Brazilian players had appeared for Portugal (Lúcio in 1960 and Celso in 1976), Scolari said:

«I accept the possibility of that happening again.»

The match against Brazil was to take place on 28 April 2003, in the old FC Porto stadium, Estádio das Antas, and as the day approached, the controversy that surrounded the affair gathered momentum and moved towards a crescendo. First of all Rui Costa, and then Luís Figo, the two main powers within the Portuguese team, both publicly declared themselves opposed to Deco's naturalisation and his consequent inclusion in the squad. As usual, Scolari reacted in his own way:

«I'm in charge of my team. If the players want to play they're welcome. If not, then they're also welcome to go. I'm not pointing a gun at anyone's head.»

And to remove any shadow of doubt, Scolari added:

«Deco is a Portuguese citizen. He has the same rights and responsibilities as any other player.»

Figo's response to these words was also very clear:

«Scolari is right. If one is not okay with it then one should leave.»

Controversy was on.

From the very early days of this situation Deco had talked with Scolari about his fear of playing one game for Portugal and then being forced to leave due to controversy and external pressure. But Scolari assured him that the only reason that Deco might not be selected was if he was in no condition to play. It would never be because someone else had decided it.

And it was Deco himself that contributed largely to calming things down. When he arrived at his first training session he told the press that he harboured no animosity to Rui Costa or Figo for the opinions that they had expressed. He believed that they both made excellent contributions to the team and the only thing that he wanted was to be able to give back to Portugal what the country had given him since he had arrived there, in his adolescence.

Figo hadn't played against Brazil before. And in the end he didn't, because of an injury picked up during training. This led to several ludicrous conspiracy theories circulating. Deco was on the bench for the first 60 minutes and then brought on to replace Sérgio Conceição and not Rui Costa, which, theoretically, would have made more sense. To his great joy, Deco scored the winning goal in his debut game… against Brazil.

Just a few hours before the game, and during the usual prematch talk with the players, Scolari had been alluding to the way the Brazilian team scored from corner kicks, showing Ronaldo's importance in the process. Without realising and certainly without intending to, Figo made an important step towards developing a very special relationship with Scolari, by being forthright in expressing his opinions. He suddenly interrupted Scolari and said:

«Please, can I say something, Mister (the Portuguese term for Boss). He might score them like that against Portugal but at Real Madrid he does it differently.»

Figo stood up and started to explain this using the images on the screen. As someone at the FPF said, «We began to win the game off the pitch.»

Given the end result, Scolari had been right to resist pressure. If he hadn't done so, he would have shown weakness and failed to gain the player's respect. For Scolari, group spirit is very important in building an excellent team.

Scolari's career is full of examples of how he will not tolerate interference in his work – something which is often mistaken as stubbornness. The most famous case is the occasion when he left out Romário from Brazil's 2002 World Cup team. The furore that resulted even led to the intervention of Brazil's President Fernando Henrique Cardoso. Nothing changed. Scolari remained firm and Romário remained out. For a very good reason. Romário, like some other important players, had asked to be excused from the America Cup so that he could have eye surgery. Scolari was then shocked to discover that having made this request Romário was, nevertheless, playing for his club, Vasco da Gama, on a tour taking place in Mexico. The result was that Romário never played for Brazil again while Scolari was in charge of the team. He always held to the belief that players should give themselves to their national team just as much as they did to the clubs that paid their wages. In the light of this stance some of his decisions regarding the Portuguese team are understandable.

In the book, *Scolari, A Alma do Penta*, the author Ruy Carlos Ostermann tells of another wonderful episode that captures the essence of Scolari's independence – something that underpins everything he does, regardless of who is paying his salary. Once, when he was the coach of the Saudi Arabian team Al Shabab, his team was losing 1-0. The Prince, who was the owner of the club, ordered him to make changes to the team. Scolari refused and told the interpreter:

«Tell him that he can be the boss at home, but I'm in charge here.»

To avoid a confrontation with the Prince, the translator purposefully misinterpreted the manager's words, but even so the Prince was suspicious. As he said, Scolari's words did not match his facial expression.

THE PSYCHOLOGIST'S HELP
NEWS FOR THE TEAM

«Some of the players didn't react as well as I had expected. I had to adapt but I also had very important assistance from Regina Brandão, the sports psychologist who drew up player profiles for me,» Scolari said, a few days before Euro 2004.

As good as he is at leading men, Scolari knows that, sometimes, he needs specialist help. Turning to a therapist was not new to him. In fact, he'd been working with Regina for quite some time in similar cases. Two days before flying to Korea for the World Cup, he met with her in order to talk about the emotional state of the squad. One of her suggestions was to put all the players in single rooms, an idea that all of them applauded. The Brazilian psychologist, who is a specialist in sports stress management, holds the view that during the major competitions, where technical, tactical and physical aspects are almost even, it is the psychological side that makes the difference.

In his diary of the 2002 World Cup, adapted by the writer Ruy Carlos Osterman, Scolari wrote, immediately after Brazil had beaten England in the quarter-finals:

«Because I had demanded a lot from the players the few days before I asked myself what I should then do. I called Regina Brandão, who helps us with the players' emotional suppport and always gives us an idea of how to bring the best out of them. I've always followed her suggestions and she always makes my work easier, as she has already worked with some of these players.»

Another episode about his friend, that Scolari mentions in the same book, relates to her intervention in the delicate case of the injury to Emerson, the very important and charismatic team captain, just before the 2002 World Cup. Scolari felt that it was a massive blow and Regina's advice proved to be of the utmost importance in dealing with the situation and removing pressure from the squad.

Once in Portugal, Scolari repeated the same formula and again requested the services of Regina. Through her various study methods and her use of questionnaires and interviews, he felt that she could help him to get to know the players in a bit more depth. It's not unusual that when people are faced with something new or unknown that there is some resistance. And so there was now amongst the players. Some even refused to collaborate with her and would not fill in the questionnaires. One of them was a well known player ... and what a player... Luís Figo! And I must say that I mention his name not because Scolari or Regina Brandão confirmed it to me – they both adhered to the strictest of confidentiality – but because that's the implication I gathered from the rest of the players.

I didn't personally see the content of the questionnaires but I know that they were intended to elicit information about several aspects of the players' personalities: their level of general education, the way that they related to each other in the team, their personal and professional motivations, and many other things. Some of the players thought these lines of enquiry were an invasion of their privacy and so they resisted for that reason. Nevertheless, their opposition was rounded on by Scolari and Regina. Even Figo's refusal was considered a personality trait, he had a kind of self-certainty which he used to deal the unknown – very much like Scolari himself in the first couple of months of work. It was also seen as a trace that affirmed the characteristics of a leader, something which was very important for the Brazilian manager. He needed to know, sooner rather than later, which players could help him both on and off the pitch, those voices that could speak for him when he wasn't around.

From the very beginning Figo's reaction was seen as a personality issue rather than one of insubordination. Actually, in the end it was Figo himself who decided to fill in the questionnaire and give it to Regina, though it was a month and a half later. Given this context, one should not find it strange that Figo turned out to be a great leader, team captain, and the voice of authority on the pitch. Not from the start though – Fernando Couto was the captain before and, out of respect for this great player, Scolari waited for the perfect opportunity before handing over the responsibility to Figo. As he did later with Pauleta and Costinha, another two players who acted as 'managers' within the group. They were also Scolari's voice. But he had so much trust in Figo that even after Figo's self imposed year's break from the Portuguese team's competitions, Scolari still gave him back the captaincy when he returned, in June 2005.

With Regina's help in drawing up the players' profiles, Scolari was able to focus on individual and collective motivation. The players became more at ease with Regina's work once they understood that Scolari's only motive was to make sure that he got the very best out of them. There was a greater purpose: the Portuguese team.

Regina's reports helped Scolari more fully understand the men with whom he was working. Jorge Andrade's confidence and constant exuberance, Ricardo Carvalho's mix of shyness and self-control, Pauleta's winning spirit, Cristiano Ronaldo's boyish but very professional way of looking at football or simply Maniche's wish to be like the players he idolised, all of these elements helped Scolari to create in Portugal the same thing that he had in Brazil: an adopted Scolari family.

*This is war,
and I have
to kill and not
be killed.*

LOSING AND LEARNING
SÉRGIO IS OUT

If Scolari was pleasantly surprised by the highly organized FPF, administered by Carlos Godinho, then, in turn, the players felt exactly the same regarding the new work methods that Scolari imposed on them.

Power point presentations, individual files – one for each player to study at home, ten minute video observations instead of two hours of watching endless games, well defined action plans which allowed the players to know in advance whether they were playing or being left on the bench. The era of players knowing whether they were in or out only minutes before the start of a game was long gone.

Another decisive factor in building trust and rapport between Scolari and his players, especially the more famous players, was that, for the first time, the players were 'forced to look up' when speaking to the manager. Whilst there was no evident lack of respect or consideration between the players and the manager, the truth is that, if only in an unconscious way, the players had always seen themselves as the stars, playing for the big clubs, earning millions and winning prestigious competitions. Not the managers. At the time, none of the previous managers had worked with a big club or won any of the major competitions. Not until Scolari. For the first time they were being managed by someone with a winning mindset, someone different. They were being managed by the world champion. Given his reputation, Scolari could easily have dealt with his players in an arrogant way but he opted for an approach which had already led him to success: he treated the players as equals though he always made sure that he was the one in charge. And because he treated everyone with respect, he expected the same in return. And when that didn't happen, he didn't hesitate to show who was the boss.

During his first year, his major 'victim' was Sérgio Conceição, a situation for which Conceição had only himself to blame. His behaviour led Scolari to lose his temper at two games in a row: in Guimarães, in a heavy defeat against Spain (0-3) and in Oslo, a few days later, when Portugal beat Norway 1-0. In Guimarães, Scolari was horrified by Sérgio's violence on three or four separate occasions during the game. Had it been a competitive match rather than a friendly then Conceição would surely have been sent off. In Oslo, Scolari ran out of patience when he heard about the foul language that the player had used with Darlan Schneider and other members of the coaching staff when he was warming up before coming on as a substitute (a substitution which in the end didn't happen because of this).

The defeat with Spain was a little humiliating and after the match Scolari found his players depressed. There was also a lot of bad feeling amongst them. Realising this, the manager said:

«It's good that we lost because this way I can understand some things I didn't before....»

He didn't need to say any more.

A month later, I had my first test as a journalist as I tried to build a relationship of trust with Scolari. Word was out that Sérgio Conceição was in an uneasy position within the Portugal team but none of the reporters were willing to write about it. I had a conversation with Scolari and because he wouldn't give a conclusive response, either one way or the other, I drew the conclusion that Conceição's days in the team were coming to an end, at least while Scolari was managing it. The editorial board at *Record*, the newspaper I was working for at the time, decided to take the risk and to run the story. And, in time, it proved to be true.

My understanding and relationship with Scolari was, to use a popular expression, not one of 'love at first sight'. As all journalists know, the relationship with their sources is something that can be beneficial to both sides. In the beginning, that's the way it worked with me and Luiz Felipe Scolari. But in time, our frequent contacts and many on and off-record conversations led me to understand that the basis of a good personal relationship can not be dependent solely on the professional side of things. As the national manager, Scolari established excellent relationships with, at least, two other reporters – my good friends José Manuel Freitas, from *A Bola* and Luís Santos, from *O Jogo*. During the press conference after Portugal's victory against Holland, in the Euro 2004 semi-final, and in a moment when his future as national manager was being talked about, he thanked the three of us personally. He then looked at Gilberto Madaíl, and said that he would happily 'remarry' the Portuguese team – and with a gesture he simulated putting a ring on his finger.

*It's a great
job but it carries
enormous responsibility.
Sometimes it is as
if it is bigger than
being Prime Minister
or President.*

DIPLOMACY TO ONE SIDE
PUSHING HIS STATUS

Luiz Felipe Scolari is someone with a long and impressive CV – his winning of the World Cup being the most famous of his achievements. Even so, he's not the type of man to push his status unless he has to. He knows, like others in his position, that he's a respected professional and there are only very few occasions when he has had to make sure that people take proper notice of him.

There's an 'invisible workload', carried out by national managers and club managers, which is very important in guaranteeing team performance. In Portugal Scolari was, on numerous ocassions, judged in the media on his selection of players, which was often controversial. But people often forget the behind-the-scenes work which has to be done and which is fundamental to success.

In January 2004 a meeting was held in Moscow to schedule the World Cup 2006 qualifying games. Carlos Godinho, Murtosa and Scolari, representing Portugal, were concerned that the Russian Federation might put pressure on the two former Soviet states – Lithuania and Estonia.

The truth is that the meeting started off on the wrong foot. The Portuguese contingent and their representatives began to fear that nothing conclusive would come from the meeting and that their concerns would not be addressed. When it began to appear that Viecheslav Koloskov, president of the Russian Football Federation and a UEFA member, was beginning to put pressure on those two countries, Scolari lost his temper and put diplomacy to one side. He reminded everybody in the room that Portugal had the best position in the FIFA rankings, and that for this reason they should be the first to suggest a schedule. Furthermore, he told them that the qualifying games involved not only Russia and Portugal and that all the teams should be given the same opportunities. Portugal were the highest ranked and he himself was a world champion. He demanded respect for both his team and himself.

The schedule of qualifying matches was finally set up in a way that pleased all the teams thanks to Scolari's words and to Estonia's strength in resisting Russian pressure.

A similar situation arose two years later, in Brussels, during the discussions for the Euro 2008 qualifications schedule. Portugal's representatives were the same, so experience was on their side. Again, a difficult meeting was expected, especially as there were several teams involved and, whilst no-one tried to take control, in reality everyone had their own interests uppermost in their minds. The meeting dragged on for three hours. When the time came for Scolari and Carlos Godinho to say their piece they were able to achieve a consensus and by the time it all ended, the two of them couldn't have been happier. The schedule was exactly the one that the Portuguese Football Federation had proposed.

ON THE BENCH
PLAYING THE REFEREES

Every manager has his own way of managing the team during the game, and dealing with the pressure of being in the dugout. Scolari just can't stand still. He can begin the match in a quiet manner but it's not long before he gets excited and it's down to Murtosa, his helping hand, to calm him down, to point out details, tactical changes, the small things that make a difference.

Scolari doesn't hide his emotions on the bench. He talks loudly, gesticulates, protests and sometimes even prays. He puts some pressure on the fourth official because he knows his status might have a little influence and may be a help in some situations. But it's not unknown for him to sometimes go a little over the top and there are some referees who don't show him any leniency, even for the smallest of slips.

The World Cup manager appreciates the role of the referee in the game and is fully aware that they are far more involved in a match than he ever can be. That's why his choice of players will, on occasion, depend on which referee has been appointed for the game. Scolari takes account of several factors – whether the player and the referee have a history – one involving previous conflicts or sending offs – or if, on the other hand, the referee is viewed as one who tends to be a little more tolerant.

All of these are things that he takes into consideration.

*Jesus said
we should turn
the other cheek.
Unfortunately,
Figo is not
Jesus Christ.*

A PRICE TO PAY
FC PORTO'S OPPOSITION

There has always been a silent and subtle opposition to the national team from FC Porto – an opposition which became particularly noticeable during a friendly game against Italy that was held in the new Estádio Municipal de Braga, when both teams were preparing in the run-up to Euro 2004.

Just before half time, Paulo Ferreira had a slight injury to his foot. Scolari asked him if he was okay to continue and Ferreira's response was clear: «Sure Mister, this is nothing.»

To Scolari's surprise, five minutes later he was told that Paulo Ferreira was in pain and wasn't able to play the second half. Only then did the manager realise what had happened: someone had received a phone call ordering the FC Porto players to stay out of the game because in a few days their team had an important match in the Portuguese league. With this in mind, he asked Costinha if he was also injured and unable to play. The 'Minister', as he's known in the team, assured him that he could count on him for as long as he wanted.

The day after, António André, a member of the FC Porto coaching staff at the time, announced:

«Our players are exhausted after playing for Portugal. It's such a disorganised team, they have to run for miles.»

It was an enlightening and revealing response.

Scolari didn't blame anyone in spite of knowing who it was that had received the phone call and passed on the orders. At the time there was only one person who was working with both FC Porto and the Portuguese team. Recognising that the individual was simply following orders from above – the orders of his main employee – Scolari decided that it was useless to point the finger at him. But when the time came to renew his contract with FPF, Scolari made sure to reorganise the medical department so as to put an end to 'collaborators' who also worked for other teams.

The heavy defeat by Italy drew attention to the most difficult period in that long preparation for Euro 2004. Portugal just weren't getting the results and the team weren't playing at all well. Unsurprisingly, Pinto da Costa, now the President of FC Porto, seemed keen to stir things up, saying to the press:

«What worries me the most is not the bad results, although those are very worrying even by themselves. What bothers me is that the players are just not performing, which is very frustrating. Scolari's choices are incomprehensible and I feel the link that existed between the Portugal team and the Portuguese people has been broken.»

Scolari stuck to his guns and ignored these comments. For him there was just one goal and he continued working towards it – taking the team to the final stages of Euro 2004. In the end, time proved him right, the Portuguese people were behind him and its team had never before achieved such excellent results in the competition.

During his first few weeks as the manager of Portugal, Scolari had approached the three biggest clubs in the country in order to meet with their managers and get to know them better. At the time I was still working at the FPF and so I accompanied him. But even this collaborative approach led to yet another controversy.

Scolari had been scheduled to visit the FC Porto training ground. Two days prior to the due date a news story appeared in the press stating that Scolari had missed a meeting with FC Porto club managers. I was in the Algarve on a Monday morning, working on a women's football competition, when I got a call from *Jornal de Notícias*, a newspaper based in the city of Porto. They were trying to find out more about the whole affair, something that was a figment of someone's imagination. I explained to them, on behalf of FPF, that Scolari hadn't missed anything at all because there had been nothing scheduled for that day. The actual meeting had been scheduled for a few days later. Still, they insisted on believing the FC Porto version of the facts, ignoring my words even though I was officially representing the Portuguese Football Federation.

On the Wednesday, Carlos Godinho called me and asked me to accompany Scolari to the FC Porto premises, in Olival, as had originally been planned, though by then everybody was aware of the 'misunderstanding'. It was 11 o'clock on Thursday when we got to Olival. No one from the FC Porto board of directors was there to meet us nor anyone from the coaching staff. We talked with José Maria Carvalho, the person in charge of the training ground about the Portugal team's training for the match that was coming up with Brazil. Then we left.

Later in a brief statement to the press, Scolari was asked why he had not planned to visit FC Porto's team in the hotel where they were staying (as they did on the evening before every match). With his natural flair Scolari answered:

«I did not visit the team because I was invited to visit their training ground and not the hotel where they normally stay. They invited me to their home knowing that they wouldn't be there.»

It was a totally different story when we went to meet Sporting Lisbon at their training ground in Alcochete. The whole board of directors was there – Miguel Ribeiro Telles (President), José Eduardo Bettencourt (CEO), Manolo Vidal (Director of Football) and Pedro Mil-Homens (Director of Premises) – to meet Scolari and the FPF delegation. It was a long and cordial visit in which

Scolari talked with some of the players, including João Vieira Pinto, who at the time was under suspension by FIFA for attacking the Argentinean referee during the match with South Korea in the 2002 World Cup, after he had been sent off. Since then, he had not been selected to play with the Portugal team.

I'm convinced that during that visit Alcochete was chosen as the national team's headquarters for Euro 2004. A choice that, in time, proved to be an excellent one.

THE 'CERTAIN' PLAYERS
AN UNUSUAL WAY TO MANAGE

One of the hardest tasks for a manager can be dealing with the egos of the players. Normally, they're excellent athletes, and most of them have international status. They are, however, shining stars in a constellation in which each struggles to outshine the others.

In the Portuguese team, the rivalry was not that problematic as most of the players had known each other since they were very young. At least, that's the way that I like to think of it. During Scolari's first years, some of the players who had been part of the so called 'Golden Generation' were still involved in the national squad and Scolari worked with them. That emotional connection to the past was still there as well as the memories of victories and of the long road to success. Today, I'm not so sure. Many changes have occurred since then and I doubt that that sense of a link with the past is still as strong.

In spite of all the professionalism that surrounds football today, the truth is that the spirit contained in a national team is still seen and understood as a clear and direct way of comparing the worth of one country to another. It is something which is beyond culture or foreign policy. And the players feel that when their national anthem echoes around a stadium before a match, they know that being there, representing their countries, is a privilege.

Scolari was brilliant when it came to managing the interests of the players and their particular vanities. He didn't resort to manipulation or to strategies such as 'divide and rule'. Quite the opposite.

One of his approaches is to clearly define a group of

'unquestionable' players – players who can always be expected to feature in his team – the 'certainties'. As long as his plans are not affected by injury or suspension, Scolari has his team well defined in his head and everybody knows it. With Portugal the players realised that to play for the team, they had to work hard and wait for their opportunity. Even when some of those 'untouchables' were not performing well for their clubs, Scolari would stick to his choices. History shows some examples, Costinha and Maniche being the most obvious ones. Before the World Cup in Germany, both had had serious problems with their clubs that could have stopped them being included in the Portuguese team. For a number of reasons, Scolari chose them and both performed in very distinctive ways during the competition. Maniche was considered one of the best Portuguese players, scoring two goals, one of which was decisive, against Holland in the last sixteen. On the other hand, Costinha, another of Scolari's 'certain' men, in the sense of his centrality to the team, proved to be a bad choice. Especially in that same game with Holland, in which he was sent off, with very serious consequences for the team.

But the clear divide between 'certain players' and 'not so certain players' did also have an impact on some of the players, particularly Tiago, Quaresma, Simão, Ricardo Carvalho and Nuno Gomes. Tiago took three years to get into the team and even then didn't manage to keep his place after that first chance; Simão was always pitted against Figo and Cristiano Ronaldo; Carvalho managed to stay in the team only after having a very impressive first game against Greece; and Nuno Gomes only became an option after Pauleta had left.

Regardless of their status, all the players were aware of and accepted Scolari's rules. Even the two icons of their generation, Fernando Couto and Rui Costa, who no longer maintained their status as Scolari's 'certain players' after Portugal's defeat by Greece in the debut match of Euro 2004.

*The club
that hires me
will become
winners...*

GOOD THINGS ARE NOT EXPENSIVE
SAYING NO TO BENFICA

During the weeks prior to Euro 2004, several news stories came out reporting that Scolari was in line to replace Benfica's manager, José António Camacho, who had been invited to become Real Madrid's manager. The truth is that Scolari, as he told me at the time, had, with the agreement of the FPF, given his personal manager, Gilmar Veloz, instructions «to listen and study work propositions».

Benfica was one of the clubs interested in Scolari, and it was a possibility that pleased him as it meant he could continue working in Portugal. Nevertheless, after Benfica's first approach, Scolari realised that things were not quite what they seemed, as the Lisbon club's financial offer was not as good as the one they had previously made to Camacho. They wanted to pay him less and Luiz Felipe wasn't at all happy with that.

«Ask Benfica,» he told his manager, «What has Camacho won in his career that I haven't?»

It is at times like this that Scolari makes sure everybody is aware of how successful his career has been. Not only was he the winner of the World Cup in 2002, as Brazil's manager, but he had also been responsible for many other victories and trophies over the years, working with Brazilian and Arabic teams and for both league teams and national teams.

In November 2002, after having refused an invitation from the Mexican Football Federation to coach their national side, Scolari said:

«Why leave Brazil to earn the same as I get here just by

speaking at conferences? If people want caviar they have to pay for caviar.»

During the Portuguese negotiation process, a reporter asked him if he was an expensive manager. Flippantly, he said:

«Good things are not expensive. Bad things are.»

But Scolari wasn't always a sharp negotiator. Far from it. When he was dealing with the second contract in his career, with Pelotas, Scolari asked for half the amount of money that the club's managers had intended to offer him. And they were so astonished that they didn't say a word. It was a silence that Scolari read as a negative response to his salary request. And so he went on to suggest that he would be willing to lower the amount. There was a second silent response and so he again lowered the proposed amount. In the end it was the club managers who had to bring the negotiations to a close before Scolari offered to work... for free! It was 1983. From then on, many things changed.

Back to May 2004, and Benfica. Scolari was, of course, right. There was no reason for Benfica's salary offer to be lower than the amount they had paid Camacho and Luiz Felipe made that very clear. Particularly because he felt that the profile Benfica was looking for in a manager fitted him like a glove. Luiz Filipe Vieira wanted someone with a «strong personality, competent, who can take the pressure and won't accept any interference in his work.»

The negotiations had reached an apparent dead end when, suddenly, rumours about Benfica and Scolari began to circulate once again. A few days prior to the start of Euro 2004, the Portuguese newspaper *Expresso*, in its online edition, ran a series of interviews revealing that an agreement had been reached between the two parties. It was a premeditated leak. Scolari attributed it to someone from inside Benfica, and felt that it was carried out with the clear intention of destabilising him and the

Portuguese team on the eve of that important competition.

Appreciating the situation, Scolari called a last minute press conference to make a statement. *Yes*, he had been approached by Benfica but *No*, he had «never signed a contract with the club».

He continued: «That's a filthy lie coming from someone with no spine and whose intention is to hurt the Portugal team. I should congratulate the person responsible for this situation. Because next Saturday, on the first Euro 2004 game, it won't be Luiz Felipe, Benfica's manager, but Luiz Felipe, Portugal's manager.»

This press conference was a bombshell and took everybody by surprise. But it had a positive effect: Scolari got everybody's sympathy and respect. Maybe that's the reason why, despite losing the first game against Greece, the public showed him their clear and solid support.

Scolari never mentioned José Veiga's name during the press conference but he was convinced it had been him, a players' agent who had just started working at Benfica. In the end, whoever it was, they were responsible for Scolari aborting negotiations with the club. At the time, despite what was written by many journalists, Scolari assured me that he had not entered into an agreement with Benfica, although negotiations had begun to run more smoothly.

Luiz Felipe interpreted this calculated leak as a strategy intended to pressure him into signing the deal. Whoever had planned it seemed to believe that undermining Scolari and troubling the Portugal team would build up the pressure and contribute to a possible defeat, which is eventually what happened. It seemed to be the view that if things went wrong for Scolari after the competition, he would be forced to sign with Benfica. In the end this turned out to be wrong. There was a wave of sympathy for Luiz Felipe, from both the players and the Portuguese public, depite the poor result of the first game.

*We have given
Portugal a day of joy.
We gave everything
we had to give.
Without this crowd
behind us and the
Portuguese people,
we wouldn't have
been able to do it.*

FLAGS IN THE WINDOWS
THE PUBLIC AND THE TEAM

More than four years have passed now since Euro 2004 but in Portugal people still seem to rejoice with the enthusiasm that was felt at the time. A special bond had been built between the Portuguese team and the Portuguese public and the country itself was decked out in green and red, with a flag in every window, on every house and on every street corner.

This 'movement' began after an appeal that Scolari made during the group stage, before the game against Russia. Portugal had to win because of the defeat they had suffered in the first game. The match was held in Estádio da Luz and Luiz Felipe knew that it was very important for the team to feel that they had the support of the Portuguese people. With this in mind, Scolari encouraged everybody to put on a Portuguese replica shirt and go to the stadium to watch their team play. Those not able to go were asked to put a flag in their window to show their support.

Scolari had no idea of what was about to happen almost as soon as he made this appeal. Although he is a master of motivation – and, like every leader, has some skills of manipulation – he never imagined that Portugal's response would be as immediate and emotional as it was, to such an extent that it wasn't long before it even became a social phenomena that was the subject of academic study. All of a sudden, Euro 2004 was visible and all-consuming, even for those who didn't like football.

The clubs were no longer important. What was at stake was Portugal and the Portuguese team. The enormity of this social phenomenon took everyone by surprise and Scolari was the first one to take advantage of it for himself. When Portugal qualified for the final, he declared that Portugal wanted to win the competition – but through fair-play. Nobody would die if we didn't win.

Portugal didn't win and no one died. But this wave of support continued even after the defeat, allowing the Portuguese people to react in an amazingly civilised way in spite of it. There was no confrontation, no controversy, there were no insults thrown, nor any of those situations which unfortunately occur with regularity these days.

LOSING = CHANGING
PLANNING AND ALTERING

Over the long period of preparation for Euro 2004, and after many games – seventeen in sixteen months – Scolari had got to know his players. He talked with each and every one of them, regardless of whether or not they had the potential to be in the final eleven or to take a place on the bench. Some he spoke to so as to find out if they could have performed better in the team, and others just to confirm the information that he had been passed on about them.

Scolari had been used to working in Brazil, the country that provides the largest number of players to clubs worldwide. The quality of the players available to the national team alone could form four or five teams of the same high quality and competitive level. Scolari soon realised that Portugal had only 14 or 15 top players. Besides them, any appointments would have to be made from amongst players who were scarcely better than average and, certainly, not a real plus to the rest of the team. And this is why Scolari quickly chose his core team and then built around it. Several experiments were made in that direction. Ultimately the candidates had to convince Scolari and his management team that they were good enough to be part of the Portugal squad for Euro 2004.

As time went on, there were still questions and doubts in Scolari's mind regarding the team structure. He felt that some of the players were not at their best, below par compared with their best performances, but that, alone, was not enough for him to drop them from the team.

His biggest doubt was not about Rui Costa, who could have been replaced by Deco, who had already proven himself to be a very reliable player and who had won the Champions League with Mourinho's FC Porto just a few days before. His biggest problem was Fernando Couto, the veteran defender who, according to Scolari, no longer had the speed or the anticipation necessary in that position. Ricardo Carvalho, on the other hand, had had a spectacular season dominating FC Porto's defence and was José Mourinho's favourite on that side of the field. Couto had been untouchable for ten years and Carvalho had only just started. And, of course, the fact that Couto was also the team captain left Scolari uneasy about removing him from the team before any big game.

One should remember the environment that surrounded Portugal's first game in the competition. The Portuguese team were the favourites – they were playing on home soil, had some of the best players in the world and, perhaps most importantly, Greece had never won a game in the final stages of similar competitions. There was enormous pressure and in the end Portugal were destined to lose! The Greeks were the outsiders, just as Portugal had been in the past, labelled as the least qualified team of Euro 2004, with the least possibility of winning. For them there were few expectations, and therefore no real pressure from the Greek public or press. In this context they were able to play a relaxed game and, consequently, to win.

Strangely enough, this first defeat provided Scolari with sufficient reason to make the changes that he had already thought about, but had kept to himself. Fernando Couto and Rui Costa were replaced by Ricardo Carvalho and Deco. Nevertheless, Costa had some pretty important moments during the competition but Couto ended his career with the Portuguese team in a way he would never have imagined – on the bench. Simão also gave way to Cristiano Ronaldo, who moved from second best to second to none, and Paulo Ferreira replaced Miguel, playing in Benfica at the time and at the peak of his career.

In spite of his injury problems, Pauleta had always been one of Scolari's certainties. He played all the games, except when he was suspended against Spain, a game in which Scolari opted for Nuno Gomes, who scored the winning goal. Pauleta remained in the team throughout the competition, in spite of his lack of goals, which underlines one of Scolari's principles: he's the one in charge of choosing the players, not the press. His decisions are based on the trust he has in key players and that doesn't change even when they're not playing at their best.

Many things were written about the changes that Scolari made after the match with Greece, and many claimed that they only happened because of pressure from the press and from the supporters. I'm still convinced that this wasn't the case. A manager like Scolari doesn't allow interference. Nor are his decisions arrived at to please others or to reach a consensus. He's a man of strong conviction and firm ideas. He knows exactly what to do and when to do it. Even if he didn't say it himself, or acknowledge it publicly or privately to his players, Scolari was ready to lose that first game. And that's the only way to explain what happened throughout the rest of the competition.

Scolari's changes didn't affect the spirit of the group, mainly because both Rui Costa and Fernando Couto, the two veterans, behaved in an exemplary manner. But it was also because of the way that Luiz Felipe handled the situation. In fact, the team got stronger. As Cristiano Ronaldo recalls in his book *Moments*:

«I remember the way we united and became a family. The Portuguese team family. And there was one person particularly responsible for this phenomenon: Luiz Felipe Scolari.»

*Now there is so
much professionalism,
we have to revert
to urging players
to like the game,
to love it, to play
it with joy.*

INFLUENCING THE PLAYERS
MOTIVATING AND OVERCOMING

While preparing for matches, Scolari is like any other top manager. He does his homework, analysing his opponents, discovering and exploring their weak points, studying details that are subtle to the untrained eye, finding in his own team solutions to overcome any obstacles. Nevertheless, Scolari always stands out as the type of manager who also believes in strengthening the emotional and psychological side of the group, both at the general and individual level.

Many people were surprised by Hélder Postiga's inclusion in the squad selected to play in Euro 2004. The young attacker had been transferred from FC Porto to Tottenham at the end of the 2003/2004 season, apparently because José Mourinho didn't see him as an option. Instead Mourinho brought in the South African, Benny McCarthy. Postiga didn't do well at the London club, which is one of the reasons that he didn't have the full trust of the fans and also seemed to be looked down on by his opponents, especially English ones. But Scolari took advantage of this when Portugal played against England in the quarter-finals. During the usual pre-match talk, he called Postiga to one side and told him:

Hélder, if I need you in the game you're going in and you're going to show them that you're better than they think. I want you to do what they think you're not qualified to do.»

Postiga got on in the last minute of the match, when Portugal were losing 1-0 and it was he who scored the goal that led to a draw and to extra time being played. By the time it came to penalty kicks, his sense of self-confidence was so high that he scored again, 'Panenka' style (named after a former Czech player who scored by chipping the ball so that its flight arched over the goalkeeper into the middle of the goal). David James, completely out of position, just watched it going in. Proving how confident he felt, Postiga had even announced to his team mate, Tiago, that if he was called on to score, he would do it that way. So, when Postiga took the ball, just before scoring the penalty, Tiago smiled and told the other players: «Check this out. It's going to be worthwhile.»

Another example, where building motivation played an important role, was with Paulo Ferreira, a naturally right-sided defender. Scolari had occasionally made him swap sides and play on the left. In one particular game in the Euro 2004 qualifiers against Belgium, in Brussels, things didn't go as planned when Ferreira, playing left-back, was partly responsible for the Belgian goal. Portugal still won 2-1 but the player was totally controlled by his opponent. Next day, in an informal conversation with some reporters on the flight to Kuwait, Scolari said:

«I've already told Paulo that for as long as I'm managing this team, he'll always be the left side defence.»

It's not easy to find a better example of how to motivate a player whose performance didn't live up to expectations.

A month before announcing his squad list for the final stages of Euro 2008, Scolari went to London to talk with Paulo Ferreira and to confirm his confidence in the player's ability, knowing that at the time he was not playing on a regular basis for Avram Grant's Chelsea. During the competition, Paulo Ferreira was, indeed, the left side defence, and Scolari left out Marco Caneira, the Valencia player who had been involved in more games for his club than had Ferreira.

Even some 'heavyweight' players needed the manager to have a few words with them. Simão, for example, questioned

Scolari's technical decisions and his choices of team captain. Basically Simão was unhappy that he himself was not playing. After a few minutes, he realised not only who was in charge of the decision making but also that Scolari clearly regarded him as a first choice and a very suitable one. Even more surprising to Simão was that Scolari also saw him as an option for team captain. In this way, the manager not only reassured the player but even added a bit of subtle pressure. The result was, as Scolari expected, positive.

Cristiano Ronaldo was told off by Scolari a couple of times. Everybody still remembers the match against Sweden in Coimbra, preparing for the Euro 2004, when Scolari threatened to leave Ronaldo out of the competition if he continued to play as an individual. The manager demanded that he should give the same level of commitment to the Portugal team as he had shown with Manchester United.

Another episode took place during the match with the Czech Republic, during Euro 2008. The match was tied. Ronaldo's first half had been a pretty mixed one – some ups, some downs, some individual displays of skill but no sign of being a team player. Scolari was furious and pointed out to Ronaldo, in front of all his team mates, that he was not the only one on the pitch – stressing what he expected from him for the rest of the match. Once again, the result was very positive. Cristiano had an amazing second half, scored once and provided an assist for another goal by Quaresma. Portugal won 3-1 and made the quarter-finals.

My name is
Luiz Felipe Scolari.
I'm not José Mourinho.
I have my own personality.
I follow my way,
not another way.

A STRONG PERSONALITY
THE TROUBLEMAKER

The portrayal of Scolari as a troublemaker stretches a long way back. The episode with the Serbian player Dragutinovic, in September 2007, led some of his critics to drag out other incidents from the past. Strangely, no one mentioned another particular incident – the time that Scolari pushed over a linesman during a match between Roma and the Brazilian team Grémio.

The manager was appalled and angered because the referee had disallowed two perfectly good goals for his team yet allowed Roma a very dubious one. Clearly it was something that he shouldn't have done yet it remained an incident that was never mentioned. Instead, as they had so many times before, they dug up incidents which sometimes weren't quite what they appeared to be.

One example happened in the Estádio José de Alvalade after the historic victory against Russia – a very impressive and expressive 7-1 victory during the qualifying stages of World Cup 2006. Four days earlier, Portugal had suffered an unexpected humiliation by drawing with Lichtenstein, after having been ahead 2-0. Team spirit was at a low ebb and as the match with Russia approached the relationship between the players and the press was tense. *Record* wrote a news story pointing the finger and raking over some obvious wounds. The story was written by Céu Freitas, a reporter who is also my sister. I have to say, as I told her at the time, I would have edited the story, changing a few words here and there to avoid anything that might cause any unnecessary reaction from the players. I texted Costinha in advance to make sure that there wasn't such a reaction, and he answered back with a positive «no worries».

But at the end of the press conference, Céu was approached in a very rude and improper way by Afonso de Melo, the Portuguese team's press officer at the time. It was totally out of order. Céu was flabbergasted and Ana Matias, a well-known Sports Marketing specialist, who was with her and witnessed the whole thing, was indignant. It was actually Ana who insisted that Céu should raise the issue with Scolari, as he was still in the building. And so she did. Luiz Felipe stopped to have a chat with her, in the presence of the police commissar Paulo Flôr. A few minutes passed by, with nothing significant happening, when Miguel Pedro Vieira, another reporter with *Record*, barged in to the conversation. Scolari lost his temper, exploded, and used some rather choice words towards Vieira. It all ended up on Portuguese TV but what was shown was only the final part of a longer saga, giving a totally wrong impression of a raging manager.

FIGO'S IN, FIGO'S OUT
A SPECIAL BOND

In spite of the frustration of their defeat in the final against Greece at Euro 2004, Scolari still managed to find renewed motivation to prepare his team for the World Cup in Germany. But it was especially difficult as he had lost two of the most important national squad players from the previous ten years: Luís Figo and Rui Costa.

The farewell announcements that each of them made couldn't have been more different – in timing, format and in what was said to Scolari.

On the eve of the Final, Rui Costa told reporters that the next day would be his last playing for the Portuguese team. He had told no one about this and it took the team and everybody else by surprise – including Scolari, who said so himself during the usual pre-match talk with the press. The relationship between the former Brazilian manager and Rui Costa had never been as close as the one he had built with Figo. Costa might have wanted to spare himself the painful task of discussing his replacement in the team by Deco, something that he thought Scolari was keen on. And perhaps that's why he didn't speak with the manager before going public.

With Figo, things were different. He had already indicated that it was his intention to quit the Portuguese team after Euro 2004, but only a month later, in a press release, he made it clear that instead of quitting he was just taking a break. It wouldn't be a definite end, although he was not ready to promise that he would make himself available again. Before the announcement,

Figo met with Scolari and told him of his intention to take some time out to think about his future.

For almost a year, the Portuguese team built its way towards the 2006 World Cup without Rui Costa and without Figo. But with Portugal's qualification becoming real, rumours began to spread that Figo might come back. And a few months later, after Glberto Madaíl had visited Figo's home in Madrid, and Figo and Scolari had had several conversations, he returned.

Luiz Felipe was delighted to welcome him back but he also told him that, out of respect for his fellow team mates, that he had to return before the qualifying stage ended and actively participate in it. And eleven months after his period out of the national side, Figo returned to play against Slovakia, in Estádio da Luz.

On 8 July 2006, after the game to determine the World Cup 3rd place postion, Figo said a proper farewell to the Portuguese team. And he did it in a very relaxed way, no drama, but clearly and confidently, like someone who's finally at peace with their decision. That day reflected the joy that he had felt during the years that he had served his country rather than the sadness of his departure.

Pauleta also left the team, but in a very different state of mind. He wasn't ready for it and couldn't avoid the commotion and tears that followed the announcement. His colleagues helped him through it, especially Figo, who knew exactly what he was going through. Once again, Scolari acted more as a friend than as a boss. And because everybody felt that there was still some uncertainty about his future with the Portuguese team, he cleared the air by saying:

«Well people, enjoy your holiday, because in September the war is on again with the Euro 2008 preparations.»

This was not the first time that there had been a doubt about

Scolari's continued position with the team. The first time had been the Benfica incident four days prior to the first game in Euro 2004 and the second was in late April 2006.

*I'm just like
anybody else,
I've got two legs,
two arms
and a head.*

CLASSIFIED INFORMATION
SHARING WITH HIS PEERS

Whenever it was convenient to him, Scolari would always excuse himself by saying that he was unable to speak English. It wasn't true. He didn't speak English fluently but he knew enough to keep up a conversation with football people. And how he loves to talk!

I witnessed this on one occasion right after Euro 2004, at a conference in Gothenburg, Sweden, a conference aimed at the managers of national teams. In spite of having lost the final to Greece, managed by Otto Rehhagel, who was also at the conference, Scolari actively participated and everybody was amazed by the down to earth and relaxed way in which he would discuss both his team's strengths and their weaknesses.

At these kind of events, Scolari tries to bond with his peers. He trades information and works towards building interesting relationships for the future. That's why he frequently talks about the information that he has received about this or that player after having spoken to 'my friends'. At other times he will be quite firm in his belief that he doesn't need to watch a certain player – that he already has enough information.

A good example of this is when he chose the Marítimo player Mukukula to play for Portugal. Sebastião Lazaroni, an old time friend, had told him:

«Listen Felipe, if you need him you can count on Mukukula. He's in great shape and can be helpful to you.»

Scolari followed his friend's advice and went to Reboleira to watch the game between Estrela da Amadora and Marítimo but the outcome was a disaster. «Don't give up on him,» his friend said and Scolari didn't. In the end it led to Mukukula playing for Portugal and scoring in the game in Almaty, against Kazakhstan.

During the first months of his reign as manager of the Portuguese team, Scolari met with some of the managers of the largest clubs in the country. Later, the FPF organized a number of group meetings, in Porto and Lisbon, as 'ice-breakers' at which Scolari told everybody to call him directly if they needed to – because he was going to do the same.

Strangely, the only club that never participated in these collective meetings was FC Porto. The excuse, in one particular case, was a little odd: «Mr. Co Adriaanse doesn't speak Portuguese.»

For a number of reasons, which are difficult to be sure of, the only FC Porto manager Scolari ever talked with properly was José Couceiro. They established such a fluid and close relationship that when, in 2006, Couceiro was invited to manage the Under-21 Portugal team, everybody thought it was because of Scolari's intervention. But Luiz Felipe had nothing to do it. When Madaíl was confronted with the situation of having to either keep or lay off Couceiro after the 2007 Under-20 World Cup in Canada, Scolari said:

«I wasn't asked an opinion when he was hired so why should I give one now he's being fired?»

A DOUBT CALLED RICARDO
A BAD PERIOD FOR THE GOALKEEPER

During the many months of preparation for Euro 2004, Scolari wasn't worried by the issue of a goalkeeper. He had Ricardo and Quim and all he was short of was a third option to complete the group. But the first name he called to pair with Ricardo and Quim generated a new controversy with FC Porto. He chose Bruno Vale, a young player who, at the time, wasn't appearing regularly. As a consequence, his choice was considered by FC Porto club managers as the ultimate insult to Vítor Baía.

For Scolari, although this issue was not a problem it was still important, and so he asked Murtosa to take a thorough look at all the available players. During the Under-20 Madeira Tournament in February 2003, Murtosa confirmed what Agostinho Oliveira and Rui Caçador had already told him: young Bruno Vale was a goalkeeper to keep an eye on. A few months later, to allow him to take a closer look, Scolari selected Vale to play against Kazakhstan.

Obviously, choosing Vale didn't help the situation regarding Scolari's non-selection of Baía and the problems that had caused. But in the end it proved an excellent opportunity for him to again make it very clear that he was the person in charge of the team. Three years later, Vale suffered an injury, a misfortune that cost him a place at the World Cup in Germany.

Scolari's first choice has always been Ricardo. Like Quim, he has spent half of his career at a small club, so he was someone who knew that he had to work hard to be able to get a chance. And when the opportunity was there for him to take, he turned in both good and bad performances – he was both hero and villain – but he never achieved the status that Baía had. During Scolari's period in charge of the Portugal team, there were some memorable performances – some bad and some good – the two Lichtenstein games, qualifying for World Cup 2006 and the unforgettable penalty saves against England during Euro 2004 and World Cup 2006. Against Lichtenstein his performance was awful and, along with Paulo Ferreira, he was responsible for the goal they scored. On the other hand, he was a decisive force, in Estádio da Luz in Euro 2004, when he not only kept out penalties but also scored one. Two years later, in Gelsenkirchen, again against England, he became the first goalkeeper in history ever to stop three penalty shots during the World Cup.

There was a moment, however, that Scolari began to doubt his choice of Ricardo, namely after Portugal's qualification for the 2006 World Cup. It was during the friendlies against Northern Ireland and Croatia. Ricardo was going through a bad spell at Sporting Lisbon, the club he was playing for at the time, and he was not playing regularly. Scolari felt it was time to give Quim an opportunity but then he got injured. Luiz Felipe felt that he had no option but to call up Paulo Santos, Braga's goalkeeper, for the first time.

While flying to Belfast, Scolari did what he always did during every flight: he stood up and greeted everybody. He then came over and sat down next to me. Our conversation lasted almost two hours and Scolari only went back to his place as the plane was approaching to land. It wasn't the kind of conversation that you'd expect between a manager and a reporter. We talked like two friends, two friends who always want their team to win. I felt that Luiz Felipe was troubled, he was worried about the goalkeeper problem at a technical level but more so at a personal one. During those two hours he confessed his doubts to me, asked my opinion about some of them, pondered measures, went back and forth on some ideas, proposed various scenarios... but in the end we just relaxed, laughed and enjoyed each other's company – and I assured him that I was not going to ask about Baía at the next press conference.

Over time Ricardo improved, and started playing regularly for Sporting Lisbon again. He kept his place in the Portuguese team. I'm not sure he was ever aware of Scolari's doubts.

*The most
important thing is to
have a unified group.
The national team
should be like
a family.*

REAL MADRID HAVE A TRY
FLORENTINO PÉREZ MAKES A MOVE

The life of a football manager is an unstable one. They're rarely in the same place for a long period of time and, sometimes, they barely get to know the countries and cities they live in before it's time for them to move on. Free time was a luxury Scolari could rarely afford during his time in Portugal but, when he could, travelling through the country and to other parts of Europe was a priority, particularly during long weekends or over the Christmas and New Year holiday periods.

One of the trips he found most enjoyable was one that he took to Switzerland with his whole family, discovering the Alps, the lakes and the ski resorts for the first time – and, of course, it was also a very different, almost exotic gastronomic experience for a Brazilian palate. The trip is one which the family will always remember. It was also perhaps inevitable that they would come across a number of Portuguese emigrants on their travels and their reaction was something that particularly touched Luiz Felipe. He found their welcome and their support deeply touching. As I have said, he is not the man that most people think he is.

There was another epsiode during that trip to Switzerland that not many people know about. Real Madrid were suffering a crisis of underperformance and Florentino Pérez, president at the time, was thinking about hiring Scolari. He managed to track down his phone number and called him a few days after Christmas. Luiz Felipe informed him he was still under contract with the FPF and wished to stay with them at least until after the

World Cup in Germany. Despite this Pérez insisted:

«I'm sending my plane to pick you up in Switzerland. Tonight we'll discuss the matter and then tomorrow you'll be back with your family.»

But Scolari declined and Pérez had to look for another option.

On another occasion, Scolari went to Italy in search of his roots. It was at the end of October 2002. When he got to the small village where his grandparents had lived before leaving for Brazil, things seemed to be going wrong. There was an air of suspicion and some of his relatives were behaving very strangely:

«We don't know anyone of your family» or «They don't live here anymore, they've all left,» they said.

In the end, it was Scolari's friend, who was also acting as his interpreter, who cleared the air, telling them that Luiz Felipe wasn't after any inheritance or land. Instead, he was a famous relative, world famous, in fact, he had just won the World Cup.

The Italians had not recognised Luiz Felipe but after this brief introduction their reaction changed – they opened their arms to welcome him in a warm embrace and invited him into their homes. They were deeply apologetic for the misunderstanding and for their suspicion. Apparently, it wasn't unknown for people to make false claims about their family background for the sake of inheritances and hence they had been cautious.

Felipe has returned to Italy many times over the years to get to understand his grandparents' country and feel in touch with it. He even has an Italian passport and dual citizenship. Scolari has joked about this. People tended to believe that the Portuguese team was run by Brazilians and yet there had never been one in charge: Flávio Teixeira, 'Murtosa', was Portuguese, Darlan Schneider was Austrian on his father's side, and then there was the 'Italian' – Scolari.

SAYING NO TO ENGLAND
A STRANGE PROCESS

In April 2006, Scolari's negotiations with the English Football Association (FA) came to an abrupt and surprising *No*, although for different reasons to the first *No* that he had given Benfica two years earlier.

The rumour that Scolari might take control of the England team had begun back in February and had become even stronger when it became public that the FA were looking for a manager to take Ericksson's place immediately after the World Cup. I had the chance to discuss this with Luiz Felipe several times and he always confirmed that whilst he knew his name was on the list that was all he knew.

The Portuguese press had almost forgotten about the whole thing until one relaxed Thursday morning. On April 27, at around noon, the bomb exploded. I was on my way to Germany to report on the opening of the hotel which was to be Portugal's headquarters for the World Cup. I had turned on my mobile and soon realised that something was happening. The news was out yet no one had known about it, not even me: Scolari had met with two representatives of the FA – Brian Barwick, Chief Executive, and a lawyer – and negotiations were moving forward at a fast pace. I called Luiz Felipe as soon as I heard. He was in Estádio do Restelo, watching Costinha's training with Belenenses, as he had left Dynamo Moscow a couple of months earlier but had still not found a club.

We talked over the phone for quite a long time and he confessed:

«Zé, nothing is final yet but I'm very tempted to accept, very tempted indeed. The problem is they want to go public with the deal, but it's not even finalised yet. I've warned them that there's a huge risk of Portugal meeting England in the World Cup. All things considered, that may really happen. It is extremely tempting but this degree of English pressure is not making things easy for me.»

During my flight to Dusseldorf, I wrote up my report for *Record's* morning edition. The story of an inevitable farewell. Barwick had already spoken to the English press and confirmed that he'd been to Lisbon to talk with Scolari, as part of the process of hiring a new manager.

The contacts between the FA and Scolari's personal manager continued over the next few days. The FA's aim was to present Scolari as the new England manager by the Thursday of the following week.

On Friday, April 28, the entrance of the small Klosterpfort Hotel, in Marienfeld, wasn't large enough to hold all of the reporters, mainly British, who were on the lookout for their big scoop. Hours earlier, departing from Lisbon, Scolari's first public statements hadn't given us any reason to feel particularly optimistic. He had made it clear that he needed to be open to every proposal or invitation (by which he was referring to the FA) because the Portuguese Football Federation hadn't yet talked to him about renewing his current contract which was due to terminate after the World Cup.

And then he had asked:

«If I'm World Champion, if Portugal has had the best results ever, then what else do I have left to prove?»

«The man is really leaving,» I said to a colleague of mine. I was absolutely convinced his time in Portugal was up.

The British media were bubbling over in their eagerness to

know what was going to happen. I managed to talk with Carlos Godinho just before lunch, while he, Scolari, Murtosa and Darlan were in Frankfurt and heading for Marienfeld. Godinho's voice became blunt and inexpressive and I realised that even while we were talking things were still being sorted out.

An hour later we texted each other twice. They had already arrived but were trying to find a back entrance to the hotel so as to be able to avoid the press. Five minutes later, I got another text from Godinho asking me to tell my colleagues from the press that Scolari was going to make a public statement at six o'clock.

The British media were in jubilant mood. They seemed convinced that Luiz Felipe was about to announce his acceptance of the FA's proposal. I told them otherwise – that if Scolari was calling a press conference without having Madaíl at his side, then surely it was not to accept it. Their personal relationship was such that it seemed inconceivable that they would do things behind each other's back. And so I was convinced that the possibility of him accepting the job was extremely remote.

At the same time, in Lisbon, Gilberto Madaíl was having lunch with Gilmar Veloz. At the end of that meal, the FPF president said something very enigmatic:

«Mr. Scolari is a professional hence he's entitled to listen to and consider any offers of work. I advise you to wait for his statement, later this afternoon.»

I knew that Scolari was going to say *No* to England even before the press conference started. When he finally showed up, with Carlos Godinho at his side, he winked at me, as he so often did. He then read a prepared statement, in Portuguese only, and wouldn't answer any questions.

The English media went berserk, particularly when they realised that they couldn't understand a word of what was going on.

*I never agreed
to anything,
my life was invaded.
My privacy was
totally under siege.*

«He just said that he's saying no to the English proposal,» I explained to one of the journalists who kept asking me to translate. Two minutes later it was all over. Scolari left the room with a throng of reporters desperately racing after him.

A very grand party was being prepared at the hotel, to celebrate its reopening after a complete refurbishment. Scolari took the opportunity to escape the press melée by mingling with hundreds of VIP guests. After the opening ceremony, Scolari disappeared into a restricted area which was off-limits to the press. With things as they stood, my colleague Paulo Calado and I decided to go back to our hotel to write up and send through our reports of the day's events.

Shortly after, my phone rang. It was Carlos Godinho:

«Zé, we left because of the British reporters but I'll pick you up outside.»

I told him I was already at my hotel but he could pick us up in an hour.

When Paulo and I returned to Marienfeld, we found some of our British colleagues still hanging around the hotel entrance. We passed through and found Scolari, Murtosa and Darlan back at the opening party, hugely happy and having great fun. Scolari looked like a new man. He was euphoric and soon he began to joke:

«Zé, have you sent your news story yet? You'll have to change it. A last minute change: having lost 'Big Phil', the English are going to try 'Mini Phil',» he laughed, pointing to his friend Murtosa.

'Big Phil' is the translation of 'Felipão', one of Scolari's nicknames in Brazil. Murtosa, a short guy, was, naturally, Mini Phil. They both laughed and I saw Luiz Felipe drinking beer, for the first time in many years. He danced, sang, talked with dozens of the Marienfeld VIPs as well as with the artists who were performing at the party. He signed autographs, had photographs taken and tasted all the German delicacies that were on offer.

But what made Scolari change his mind so quickly? Again, it was the press. In Portugal, in spite of everything, he had found that it was a civilised environment where the press respected his privacy and that of his family. They didn't harass him on his doorstep. The previous 48 hours, Luiz Felipe had begun to understand what he might be getting himself into:

«It was terrible,» he told me, «On Friday night I had a battalion of reporters waiting at my door, annoying my neighbours, scaring Fabrizio, pressuring Olga to pick up the phone or come to the door. And then, when we were in Frankfurt waiting for our flight here, I read all the rubbish that the British press had written comparing Olga's clothes to those of Eriksson's partner – what they do, which hairdresser they go to – and I don't know what else! What is this? If they want to compare me to Eriksson it's fine but what does Olga have to do with it? Our life style? What my boys do? I realised that I was not going to put up with that and I said to Murtosa and Darlan: 'I'm not going'. They answered like good friends: 'Felipe, you decide and we'll follow you.' I gave them and Godinho a hug.»

But there was still more to come. The FA had allowed the British press access to some important information about their first approaches to Scolari, documents which described the unfinished process, and which outlined their unacceptable deadlines. They kept nothing secret. No one with any common sense tries to hire a manager only two months before the World Cup and then leaks information about it. Even worse was trying to force an agreement before the competition had started, when there was a clear risk that the two sides might meet during the competition. For Scolari there was a clear conflict of interest. But not, apparently, for the FA who acted not only in a nonsensical way but also in an unethical one. Its representatives seemed to believe that no one would ever refuse the chance of working with the England team, something which showed a complete lack of awareness or proper research into Scolari's personality. He had made it clear that he didn't intend the matter to even become public let alone have an agreement announced.

That afternoon, 28 April 2006 in Marienfeld, after he announced his rejection of the offer, Scolari confessed to me his disappointment at the FA's behaviour:

«Zé, how is it possible to work like that? If you want to hire a manager who is employed by another national side, a matter of weeks before the two countries could play against each other in the World Cup finals, then you just can't behave in the manner that they did. Their public statements show a total lack of responsibility! When we met in Lisbon I had to inform Madaíl, because they didn't have the courtesy to ask the FPF's permission to approach me. These guys think that because they're the FA that they can do whatever they want? Zé, it was a very good proposal. I would have been the first Brazilian manager ever to work with two European teams. But I told them: 'You cannot reveal anything before the World Cup, even if the FPF knows, because there's a good chance that Portugal and England will meet each other after the group stage.' But they didn't care and they have only themselves to blame. Them and that immense, speculative press that makes up unbelievable things without caring about the truth.»

Meanwhile, in England, the way that the FA had conducted the whole process was criticised from many different quarters, including a former manager, Howard Wilkinson, who said the whole case reminded him of an episode of Monty Python.

Some have speculated that it was money that drove Scolari away from taking on the role of England manager. But that theory doesn't make any sense. After all, the FA offered him several times more than he was currently earning through his salary and through his lectures and advertising deals.

«Money is important,» he says, «but it's not decisive any more. The money was important when I went to the Middle East and then Japan, but not any more. Now we are independent. We are fortunate enough to be able to choose where to work and live and I cannot force my family to make any more sacrifices for my career.»

Over recent years, Scolari has received some good financial offers: Barcelona, Fenerbahce, Chelsea (the first approach was made in April 2007), Paris Saint-Germain (before and after coming to Portugal), Real Madrid (in December 2005), Brazil, England and Australia (a week after renewing his FPF contract at the end of the World Cup 2006). This is why I believe that it's true when he tells me that money is not everything.

When Scolari started work with the Portuguese team, he was already used to the demands that would be placed on him as manager of a national team. Nevertheless, just like any other manager, he still felt the pressure and the tensions: the daily decisions, the weekly planning, the endless game preparation, the management of the players and the conflicts that can arise because each of them believe themselves to be the most important.

In a national team, time, rhythm, tension and pressure are different. Things can be planned more than once, decisions can change over time and the players are less likely to need emotional support. His experience with the Brazilian team was an indication of what to expect. There, a year that had started out in turmoil had ended with a world title.

Once in Portugal, Scolari began work with an 18 month contract, added two more years and then two more. His way of life and of work was quieter, more private and more relaxed. He got used to it and he liked it. By the end of Euro 2008, Scolari had worked for five and a half years with the Portuguese team. And never before had a manager achieved so much with the Portuguese team, which is why, when we talk about Portugal, we should talk about 'before Scolari' and 'after Scolari'.

In the last thirty years only one other foreign manager has accomplished anything similar in Portugal: the Swedish manager Sven-Göran Eriksson, who arrived at Benfica, for the first time, in 1982. Both Scolari and Erikkson changed the way of thinking and of working, because of their particular ability to communicate, especially with the players. They think about football as being more than just running and scoring, and ultimately they both brought a fresh, ambitious and winning spirit to Portuguese football.

Two other managers, both Portuguese, have also left their personal mark on the game – although for very different reasons: Pedroto and Mourinho. Two 'conflict' managers, masters of the backstage war and of psychological struggles. They belonged to different eras but both have broken down barriers of preconception about their club – a club where they were both household names, FC Porto. Both are united by the same warrior spirit. A staged one, obviously. But in spite of being 20 years apart, they're an example of managers who used language, speech, and especially the Media as a means to an end.

And that goal was clear: helping their team to win.

*You play with joy
when you get
the right result.
How can you play
with joy if you lose?*

THE WORLD CUP SQUAD LIST
A RISKY ANNOUNCEMENT

For more than five years I managed to hold onto a privileged position of being able to release exclusive stories about the Portuguese team. The most notable one was in relation to Scolari's team selection for the 2006 World Cup in Germany.

Two years earlier, for Euro 2004, I had been unable to anticipate exactly the names of the 23 players who were finally selected for the squad. And so I did the same as everybody else: I published a list of 26 players but still missed three names. I didn't want to make the same mistake again.

My biggest doubt lay with Quaresma. Most of the commentators had called for his inclusion in the squad list, but I knew that Scolari wasn't convinced. I also questioned myself about who was going to replace the unfortunate Jorge Andrade as well as two or three other minor doubts. But I had another situation to deal with. Scolari was announcing his list on Monday while Agostinho Oliveira, the Under-21 manager, was doing it two days before. Meaning, that as soon as he released it, everyone else would be able to guess Scolari's.

My mission for those two weeks was to try and find out the names that would make up Scolari's list. It was a challenge that I set myself, with my editor's agreement, although we both feared failure. A justified fear: one wrong name and all of it would have been in vain. And it almost was.

I started preparing a few days prior to the due date by having several conversations with Scolari. I told him of my intentions and we defined a model through which I could build my list without receiving a clear 'yes' or 'no' from Scolari's lips. I could ask him to comment within specific guidelines, profiling some of the players or describing positive or negative characteristics. The conclusion always had to be mine.

Monday, May 8, late afternoon, I thought my list was closed and ready to publish. For a few hours, we even considered publishing it in the next day's edition, Tuesday, but, at that time, we didn't have any free space and so it was decided to hold it over for the Wednesday. And I'm very glad we did because one of the names was wrong. In fact, on the Tuesday, when I was doing a final proof read of my list I called Scolari to inform him that we were publishing the story the next day. For some reason, I don't recall, I talked to him about Tonel and his silence led me to think he wasn't on the list. Then I asked Scolari:

«Felipe, without breaking the rules of our agreement please tell me: is Tonel on the list?»

Scolari's silence, once again, assured me that he wasn't. I hung up the phone, looked at my notes and at the 25 names (Quaresma wasn't included at that point) and, all of a sudden, I figured it all out. It wasn't difficult for me and it shouldn't have been for anyone else who had paid close attention to his work and comments over the last few years: the defensive midfielder who would be substituting Jorge Andrade was not Sporting Lisbon's Tonel, but Ricardo Costa, the FC Porto player. It confirmed my earlier thoughts about Quaresma. I felt sure he was not one of Scolari's selections.

On the day that Scolari released his list, everybody already knew that Quaresma had been selected by Agostinho Oliveira for the Under-21 team. Some of my colleagues down at the FPF headquarters made jokes about my presence there as I had already published what I thought would be the list. But the truth is, although I had confidence in my work, a last minute change could have easily ruined my predictions.

When the names of the 23 players were being unfolded, I felt both a growing relief and the eyes of my colleagues on me. When it was all over and the complete squad list had been announced the 23 names I had published in *Record* the week before were the same as Scolari's. At that very moment two of my colleagues, António Magalhães and Bernando Ribeiro, sent me a text and congratulated me.

I don't have the slightest problem acknowledging that I felt rewarded. The day before I had read a few articles filled with innuendo, provocation and envy coming from people who insist on identifying me as the 'former FPF and Scolari press officer'. They forget – because they know that repeating a lie ten thousand times makes it true – that I had already been a journalist for twenty years when I started working with the FPF. And, whilst there, I worked alongside Scolari for only four months.

Strangely, two of those small-minded critics have the same surname – Santos – but neither of them is my friend Luís Santos, a huge man and a great reporter.

*My problem
is I'm stupid,
I tell the truth
while others lie.*

A DILEMMA AT THE WORLD CUP
A FAMILY AFFAIR

Germany's World Cup was reaching the end and Scolari's future was still unknown. Gilberto Madaíl kept saying everything was running as it should be, but after talking with the manager a few times I still had strong doubts. With this in mind, I was, once again, forced to take risks for myself and *Record* by reading between the silences. With Scolari's agreement, I made it my priority to gather exclusive stories from an unquestionable source: Luiz Felipe.

The day I published a story saying that Scolari's future was unclear and that he was considering taking a sabbatical after the World Cup, the *O Jogo* newspaper reported that he had already agreed to renew his contract with the FPF for two years. António Magalhães, *Record's* sub-editor, called me and I assured him that my story was based on information from Scolari. Still, as soon as I hung up, I called the manager. It was early in the morning but he agreed to talk to me for a few minutes and reassured me:

«Zé, nothing is definite yet, it's quite the opposite. Don't worry about the story. Did I ever fool you?»

Of course not.

The report that *O Jogo* released made sense only because their journalists were also close to Scolari and to some of the FPF members. Furthermore, Joaquim Oliveira, besides owning the newspaper, also dealt with sponsorship issues for the FPF and was always well placed with his business contacts. Later I learned that some of the most prominent financial gurus involved with the larger companies had tried to use Joaquim Oliveira to contact Scolari and 'tie' him into a new contract.

A few days later I went back to the same matter and wrote that Scolari was leaving. It was total mayhem, even for the FPF's president himself, who called me to check whether I knew something that he didn't. During that phone call, we were more like two friends talking to each other rather than a president and a reporter. In the end, I was fully convinced that Madaíl was not even 50% sure that he could hold on to Scolari. Given the informal and friendly tone of our conversation, I told him I didn't mind being wrong that time. But on the same day, I also realised that things were not as clear as I had previously thought which is why I'd decided to have another go at the same story. I wrote that I thought that Scolari's departure was inevitable. It was the same day that Portugal challenged for third place in the World Cup, against Germany, much like 6 years earlier, when Portugal had been managed by Humberto Coelho.

That afternoon I got another phone call from Gilberto Madaíl, but this time it was a far from friendly one. It was a tough conversation, we both yelled at each other, I had to endure some accusations that were neither pleasant nor true. He told me that I was collaborating with Scolari's manager and that our plan was to publish reports about Luiz Felipe that would add to the pressure and add value to his contract. I was in the press room of the Stuttgart stadium and some of my colleagues there couldn't believe what they had heard.

Before hanging up, I told the FPF's president:

«Mr. Madaíl, I repeat what I said yesterday: I hope my news story is wrong because I feel that Scolari's leaving is a great loss for the team but I also feel that this line of conversation will get us nowhere.»

A few days later, and in spite of a FPF statement which appeared on their website on July 24 about Scolari's contract renewal, a series of facts began to emerge which suggested that my report was the one closest to the truth. In fact, on July 7, Scolari had received a phone call from Ricardo Teixeira, the president of the Brazilian Football Federation (CBF), inviting him to return to Brazil to work with their national team. They had arranged to meet in person, the following Tuesday, July 11, in London, although they had first considered meeting in Barcelona.

When Scolari and the Portuguese delegation were on their flight back from Germany on Sunday, July 9, Scolari thought it would be his last time travelling with his players. But when he got home, everything changed when he raised the subject with his wife, Olga. Her decision was final: going back to Brazil? No way!

Two years earlier, with Euro 2004 still to come and Scolari's future again uncertain, Felipe had lived through another tense family situation. His oldest son, Leonardo, had told him:

«Dad, if you want to go and work in another country it's fine, no problem, but I'm staying.»

Leonardo was doing well in his Law degree and was the first family member to consider Portuguese life as a long term option rather than merely a temporary one. Today, Leonardo is an intern in of the most prestigious law firms in Lisbon.

At the time, Luiz Felipe explained to me a little about his state of mind. We had gone to Alcochete, Sporting Lisbon's training academy:

«Zé, these are the moments which are an epiphany – when you realise you're old. When your oldest son tells you to get on with your life, that he'll stay exactly where he is, it's like taking a punch in the stomach. You become speechless and realise that life passes by very quickly. It was a really hard thing to acknowledge!»

Scolari's decision was inevitable: he stayed in Portugal and continued his work with the national team. But it wasn't a hard decision to make, not least because his manager, Gilmar Veloz, and Gestifute, the company that manages his advertising and commercial deals, had already taken care of the contract renewal. Scolari was very happy, mainly because he felt that his family were not being forced to make any more sacrifices for his career.

On Sunday morning, 10 July 2006, Scolari called Ricardo Teixeira and cancelled the appointment they'd scheduled for the next day, in London. The mighty CBF president still tried to convince him but it was too late, though some behind-the-scenes rumours tell of another form of agreement between them, a deal that's not confirmed by Scolari – this suggests that Ricardo Teixeira agreed to choose a manager of whom Scolari approved so that the door could be left open for him to return before the 2014 World Cup, which is to be held in Brazil.

In the end, what's funny about all of this is that on Friday, July 14, hours before the FPF announced the renewal of Scolari's contract, *O Globo*, a Brazilian newspaper based in São Paulo, published the whole story about Luiz Felipe and Ricardo Teixeira's conversations, confirming what I'd written in *Record* the week before: by the time that Portugal met Germany, Scolari was already prepared to leave the Portuguese team.

THE BATTLE OF NUREMBERG
TEAM SPIRIT

While he was coach of the Portuguese team, Scolari oversaw 74 matches, 43 of them were competitive and the others friendlies. It's more or less commonly agreed that, during this period, the best display by the Portuguese team was against Russia, in Alvalade, a qualifying game for the 2006 World Cup. A striking 7-1 win against a powerful opponent! What more can a team offer its manager?

«It was a very beautiful game, spectacular, it's not every day you score so many goals against such a group of players like Russia,» Luiz Felipe acknowledged a few days later.

Yet in a recent interview given to Afonso Melo (*Weekly Jornada*), Scolari stated that the game he'll never forget «the most amazing of all, the one I'll tell my grandchildren about, was in Nuremberg, against Holland, during the 2006 World Cup.»

And knowing Luiz Felipe it is easy to understand why. The reasons he gave, in the same interview, are worth repeating:

«That day Portugal played like a real team! A team! As a whole! And when I say team I'm not just talking about the players on the field. I'm talking about everyone; each and every one of us in Nuremberg made up an exceptional team. That time I felt I had a group ready to help me, to help each other. Players, managers, the whole staff. We were as one.»

The Franken-Stadium – less that a kilometre away from the buildings in which Leni Riefenstahl filmed Adolf Hitler during the Nazi period – was dressed in orange. It seemed completely full of Dutch supporters. The few Portuguese present were secretly praying for a good performance from Scolari's 'pupils' so as to dampen down Dutch expectations.

Luiz Felipe knew it would be a difficult test; «maybe the hardest if we want to get to the Final,» he admitted in a press conference. Holland had a powerful attack and were a highly effective and efficient team. But on the other hand, Portugal also had several cards to play: the quality of Figo, Cristiano Ronaldo, Deco or Maniche, plus the coolness and reliability of Petit and Costinha and, of course, the group spirit that Scolari had inspired. For two days Scolari explained Holland's weaknesses, pointed out the permeability of their defence when pressured from the wings or from centre-field with the ball to feet.

What Scolari wasn't expecting was the opponents aggressiveness or the referee's soft approach. The Russian referee, Valentin Ivanov, later admitted that he had been under some Dutch pressure not to pay any attention to the «sneaky and unethical Portuguese tricks.»

The 'Battle of Nuremberg' actually started backstage. When the Portuguese bus arrived at the stadium, Scolari and Carlos Godinho were told by António Gonçalves, the team's kit-man, that something strange was going on – he had seen the Dutch management going into the referee's locker room. António is always the first to get to the stadium premises, normally an hour before, as he has to have everything ready before the players arrive. Godinho joined him as quickly as he could and once in the stadium he saw Harry Been, General-Secretary of the Dutch Football Association, leaving an area which, according to FIFA and World Cup regulations, was forbidden to him.

When asked why he had entered such an area, Been replied that he had gone to pay the referee his compliments and also to offer a symbolic gift. Although it seems strange, these gifts are a fairly standard procedure – but not before the match, only after.

Godinho wasn't happy with what he heard and immediately asked to talk to the FIFA delegate, Paulo Mony Samuel, from Malawi. He, in turn, condemned the Dutch behaviour. He also informed them that he would be mentioning the incident in his report and he put the referee's locker room under strict security.

This incident prepared Scolari for the worst. And he was right. The match had barely started when Mark van Bommel stamped on Cristiano Ronaldo's foot from behind yet the referee only gave him a yellow card. Seven minutes had passed, and Ronaldo again was severely kicked this time by Khalid Boulahrouz. He also only received a yellow card. From a Portuguese perspective, the referee seemed to be acting in a way that was favouring the Dutch players. He was ignoring their strong challenges. Cristiano Ronaldo on the other hand was becoming increasingly fragile and after only thirty-seven minutes he was substituted by Simão. Ronaldo's tears were ones of both desperation and anger and, of course, everybody knew what appeared to have gone on before the match.

It was a very tough game, full of endless provocation. A match that forced Portugal to be at their best, concentration was essential, but of course, mistakes were still made by the Portuguese team, especially Costinha, who touched the ball with his hand after being shown a yellow card. He was the first of four players to be sent off during the 'Battle of Nuremberg'.

Match statistics appear to confirm the referee's double standards: the Portuguese team committed ten fouls and received seven yellow cards in total. Two of their players received second yellow cards and were therefore sent off.

In effect, therefore, only three of the fouls committed by Portugal didn't result in a card! The Dutch, who were seen as having started the hostilities, committed 15 fouls and were only shown 5 yellow cards in total with two of their players being sent off after receiving two further yellow cards.

What was the secret ingredient that saved the night for Portugal, besides the extraordinary goal scored by Maniche that gave them victory? An indomitable group spirit, a winning mindset, a strong will to overcome adversity and not fearing the opponent. It was as Scolari once said in an interview in April 2004:

«Playing for the national team is like going to war and fighting for your country.»

Months later, in a ceremony held in Santarém, the sculptor José Coelho offered Scolari a piece that he had entitled 'The Battle of Nuremberg'.

Talking about it later, Scolari said:

«I'm going to keep it for the rest of my life as it symbolises that magnificent game I'll never forget. Regardless of the many titles I may win as national manager, having won that extremely difficult battle is the biggest title.»

THE GEESE AND THE TEAM

Scientists have discovered the reasons that geese fly in a 'V' formation:

They can fly 71% further than when flying alone.
Acting within a team the player is stronger than he is by himself.

When a goose leaves the 'V' it feels the air pressure more strongly.
It's easier when a team plays in a structured and organised way.

When the leader goose is tired it goes to the back of the 'V' and gives its place to another goose to drive the group forward.
A team needs to be committed and everybody needs to play their part to win.

The geese at the back motivate the ones in the front.
Motivating team mates on the pitch is as important as scoring or defending a penalty.

When a goose is injured two others help it and then fly on together.
Raising the moral of a team mate who has made a mistake is of utmost importance for the team's ultimate goal.

(from *Scolari, A Alma to Penta,* a lecture given before the Brazil-Belgium match during the 2002 World Cup)

I am what you see.
I like to play, I like jokes,
but my wife knows me best
– get in touch with her.

FAMILY LIFE
THE UNKNOWN SIDE

One of the biggest difficulties Scolari felt he faced in his everyday life has to do with the way that Portuguese people drive. As a family man, Scolari has always driven safely, and he found good reason to be a little scared by some of the 'outrageous' things he saw while he was in Portugal.

«You drive in a suicidal way!» he confessed to me.

On the highways, Luiz Felipe doesn't go above 110 km/hour (the speed limit is 120 km/hour) even when he is driving high powered cars. He found his first days of driving in Portugal absolutely terrifying as he watched others pass him by at 200 km/hour during his daily trip between Cascais and Lisbon.

But if adapting to the Portuguese way of driving wasn't easy, training his palate to Portuguese food wasn't either, especially when it came to fish. Like any true 'Gaúcho', what Scolari really likes is meat and a good barbecue. Scolari knew it would be difficult to find some of his favourite Brazilian products in Portugal but delicious parcels would arrive from his hometown in order to keep the barbecue running. The first months of Scolari's family life were not particularly adventurous on the gastronomic front but slowly, step by step, they educated their taste buds to Portuguese food and in the end became used to it, though when he was not at home, Luiz Felipe was still very happy to trade the usual espresso for a tea.

Overall though, settling into the Portuguese lifestyle wasn't difficult for the Scolari family. Choosing a spacious apartment in Cascais, with a fabulous sea front, and near all the amenities, was their first step. Felipe likes to keep Olga company at the supermarket and they soon met some of their neighbours. Their sons' schools were another important issue for the Scolari family. Leonardo, the oldest, enrolled in a private university to take a Law degree, while Fabrizio, the youngest, started school near home, close to Estoril.

Scolari spent much of his free time at home. Working with a national team is not as demanding as working for a club, in terms of the schedules and training days, and so he was given the opportunity to repay Olga and the boys by giving back some of the time and attention that he had not been able to provide previously, especially during the 1990s.

The first occasion that they were apart for any length of time was the most difficult and happened when Scolari went to Kuwait. He was entering a whole different world and a different culture and his wife was staying behind in Brazil. But financially it was worth it for them and Olga gave him all the support that he needed.

When Luiz Felipe went to work with the Emirates team he knew that the job would demand a lot more patience than anything else he'd done before, not least because the football culture was very different. But he was given all the resources he needed and, at end of the day, working away from home paid off both financially and in terms of his career. His Kuwaiti bosses certainly did all they could to please their manager.

His worst moment came with the invasion of Kuwait by Saddam Hussein's Iraqi troops. At the time, the team was in Vichy, (the spa town in France), preparing for the Asian Games. For the first two days, the only thing on the minds of the players and the officials was to get some news about their families back home in Kuwait. Scolari and Murtosa's very human qualities were later remembered with much appreciation by both officials and players: they had proved to be a shoulder on which to lean, and on which to cry – a great support for those saddened and anxious about the future of their families and country.

After three or four days, the Kuwaiti managers were forced to conclude that, because of the new political circumstances, they could no longer keep on Scolari and Murtosa and they felt forced to let them go. The officials said that they would make sure that they got paid everything to which they were entitled. Luiz Felipe told them that the money was not important and when he left he never actually thought he would get it. In the end though, after the social and political situation had calmed down, both were paid every last penny, part of which was donated by Scolari to a local charity. Almost sixteen years later, when Scolari and Murtosa went back to Kuwait with the Portuguese team, a party was held for them organised by 18 of the 22 players they'd worked with in the past.

The second experience away from the family, a year later, took him again to the Middle East, this time to manage Al-Ahli, in Saudi Arabia. As a husband and a father this relocation was a true nightmare. Olga was pregnant with Fabrizio, who was due shortly. After the qualifying match for the Emir Cup, it was planned that Scolari would pack up and fly home to Brazil to be with his wife. But the relative of an Emir died and, in keeping with tradition, the country was thrown into mourning – the period of which was to be two weeks. As a result everything was delayed and Scolari was forbidden to leave the Emirates. He tried to insist, telling them he would be back in time for the matches but still they wouldn't allow him to leave the country, and as they were holding his passport he had no choice.

Saddened by the whole affair, Luiz Felipe called Olga. It was she who in the end managed to cheer him up, telling him that everything would be okay for her and the baby. Next, Scolari called the doctor, a long time friend, and opened his heart to him:

«You know that Olga is due next week. I can't be there to assist her but please take good care of her.»

The doctor reassured him, Olga had an unproblematic delivery and three weeks later, Scolari met little Fabrizio.

«He's just like you,» he told Olga, glowing. And it's true.

Whenever they can, Scolari and his family travel around Portugal to visit new places and to meet its people. They love Minho, especially the Guimarães historic centre, but also the Algarve, Aveiro, Porto and anywhere they feel that they've discovered new things that they haven't seen anywhere else in the world. During their free time and over short holidays they try to escape the photographers and TV cameras. Even in the liveliest places on the Algarve they look for relaxation and privacy. Social life and its associated activities have never worried him but neither have they been a priority.

It was during those travels around the country that Scolari began to realise how popular he was amongst Portuguese people in general. During his first few months in post, when the first critics began to raise their heads, that support was crucial to him, enabling him to carry on working in the same way that he had always done: as the one in charge of his team.

A WORD OF APROVAL
TESTING A PLAYER

The relationship between Scolari and the biggest Portuguese clubs was very much an up and down affair, a situation that wasn't entirely Scolari's fault. The open hostilities with FC Porto, which began as soon as Porto realised that the national manager couldn't be controlled, ended up setting an inevitable pattern for future difficult relationships between Luiz Felipe and FC Porto managers. The first episode was one which involved José Mourinho but many others followed after Mourinho himself had left for Chelsea.

I remember, for instance, that the FPF set up a few meetings between Scolari and the clubs that provided players to the Portugal team. The only club which had no representation at those meetings was FC Porto, who justified their absence by saying that their manager didn't speak Portuguese. Not even Rui Barros, a key member of the coaching staff, was authorised to go. Even with José Couceiro, with whom Scolari had a cordial relationship, their official contacts remained non-existent, although they spoke on the phone regularly.

Paulo Bento, from Sporting Lisbon, was the closest to Scolari and on numerous occasions they would exchange ideas and information about certain players. Carlos Martins was one of them. A player that both managers tried to help several times. At the start of the qualifying stages of Euro 2004, Scolari selected Carlos Martins for the first time, even though a number of people were sceptical and had advised him against it. A conversation with Paulo Bento had removed his doubts:

«You won't regret calling him up to the team.»

But Martins almost blew it when he turned up injured after the match with Denmark and thus unable to train until the Finland game. Scolari felt let down. After all, those who accused the player of a degree of emotional instability, of 'making up' injuries, were perhaps right. Even so, Luiz Felipe didn't give up on him. Months later, and in spite of Martins going through a bad period at Sporting, Scolari put his trust in him again.

He called Paulo Bento and said:

«Look Paulo, I don't want to interfere with your work at Sporting but I'm tempted to select Carlos Martins again. If I do, will it harm the club?»

Paulo's answer couldn't be clearer:

«Not at all Felipe, on the contrary. If you do it he may realise there's more people that like him than he thinks.»

And so Scolari selected Carlos Martins once again, but once again he was not convinced. A third attempt was made, a few months before Euro 2008, at a time when Martins had shown some modest improvement at Recreativo de Huelva, in the Spanish league, but it still didn't work out and in the end the player wasn't selected by Scolari for the competition.

AFTER LUÍS FIGO
AN ADOPTED 'SON'

During the preparations for Euro 2004, Scolari discovered a true diamond in the raw: Cristiano Ronaldo. Immature, exuberant, a selfish player but also a prodigy as far as technique and skill were concerned. This was Ronaldo, 18 years old, who had just moved to Manchester United. Just like Sir Alex Ferguson, Scolari knew he had to be patient with Ronaldo, help him grow as a man, polish him as player, work on him like a master jeweller might.

Evidently, much of that work had been done by Alex Ferguson and, especially, Carlos Queiroz, but for the few days that Scolari lived with Ronaldo during the Portuguese team's preparation, he took the opportunity to get to know him, to talk to him and to make him see, that although he was an exceptionally talented player, in the team he would be just another member.

Luís Figo had a silent part in Cristiano's evolution. The position of right wing belonged to him as did the number seven shirt. Cristiano was given the number 17 (the second number seven, the second Figo), whilst Deco took number 20 as the number 10 shirt rightfully belonged to Rui Costa.

Figo's attitude towards Cristiano was more like that of a captain and team mate than of a veteran leader preparing his replacement. Ronaldo looked up to Figo as an idol but he also had the attitude of someone who was ready to take on the mantle and be even better than him. And Figo knew it. In time destiny would give Cristiano his number 7, and the attention and the praise would go entirely to him. That's the law of life, especially in the implacable football world. Nevertheless, even though his future looked bright, Cristiano's first two or three years in the Portuguese team were not easy as he was forced to wait until Figo's career had come to an end before he was able to open a way for himself. And that's exactly the point at which Scolari took command and moulded Cristiano's role within the Portugal team.

He started to prepare him to deliver important performances, not just for the actual matches. In spite of his youth and his consequent immaturity, Scolari began to coach him to become team captain. And he was captain, for the first time, in a friendly game. It was against Brazil, in London, at the Emirates Stadium, February 2007. All the symbolism associated with this match, the opponents and the consequent media exposure led Scolari to decide that he should choose this match to hand Cristiano that responsibility. Portugal beat Brazil for the second time in 40 years (and also the second time that Scolari had been in charge of the team). Cristiano was one of the best players and the team started to get used to a new leader, a future captain.

After the strong bond that had been created with Luís Figo, Scolari discovered a 'second son' in the Portugal team. He helped Ronaldo grow as a player and become a symbol of the team. Now, after ending this period of his life as Portugal's manager, he leaves with a certainty: he has helped another highly skilled player find his place amongst the 'big fish' of world football.

But it wasn't easy. Even nowadays, Scolari remembers the day that he met Ronaldo, an adolescent always wearing a baseball cap turned back to front (something he never took off, not even when eating at the table...), large sunglasses and headphones with such loud music one could hear it from a distance. Like any other adolescent, he was convinced that he was the centre of the world and couldn't care less about the advice of any manager. For months, during the Euro 2004 preparation games, Scolari felt that there were some communication issues:

«I don't think he understands what I say,» Luiz Felipe complained to me a few days before he publicly told him off in Coimbra, at the Portugal-Sweden match.

«He's a good kid but someone must have told him he's the best in the world. And if he actually thinks that it will be very hard to work with him.»

In his book *Moments*, Ronaldo says:

«With Scolari I've established an amazing relationship and I can say we're truly friends. I've always had good advice from him in matters related to football but also in some private issues. I will never forget the conversation he had with me when my father died.»

Ronaldo was in Moscow with the Portuguese team, for the match against Russia, on the eve of Portugal's qualification for the 2006 World Cup, when Scolari called him to his room. He and Luís Figo, team captain, told him that his father had died and authorised Ronaldo to leave immediately. But Ronaldo wished to stay and play as a homage to his dad.

«This was the moment my bond with Scolari became stronger. We both cried when he told me the story of when his own father died.»

A few years later, when Luiz Felipe handed Ronaldo the captain's armband, it was a premature but intentional decision. As Scolari told me a few days after that first game with Ronaldo as captain, in London, against Brazil, in February 2007:

«Zé, one day you have to let your children go and let them move on with their life. With Cristiano it is the same thing. It's time he takes on the team leadership. Maybe it's a bit early but he has to do it. I need him to be able to accept responsibility within the group. I believe that being a captain will enable this and will help him on his path.»

ALWAYS A DOUBT
IS QUARESMA INCOMPATIBLE?

Ricardo Quaresma and Cristiano Ronaldo are two of the best players in the world in their particular positions. According to some of his critics, Scolari made a mistake by not calling up Quaresma for the 2006 World Cup. Especially because the player was at the peak of his performance, developing well with the support of Co Adriaanse, FC Porto's manager, during the 2005-2006 season.

The pressure continued even when Scolari began to select the young player regularly. The truth is that Scolari never believed that Quaresma was good enough to substitute Simão, let alone Cristiano Ronaldo. His performances were unpredictable, he was not a team player nor was he consistent when playing against strong opponents. In the attack quartet (Cristiano Ronaldo, Simão Sabrosa, Nani and Quaresma) he was the weakest link. There's no doubt that he scored an amazing goal in the victory against Belgium, in Alvalade, as part of the qualification for Euro 2008, but that was it.

Almost five years after his debut with the Portuguese team, in August 2003, Quaresma was still a puzzle to Scolari as far as the best way to set up effective communication between player and manager was concerned. It seemed that he simply ignored Scolari's words. The contrast between him and Cristiano Ronaldo couldn't have been greater, as Scolari confided to me on more than one occasion.

And during the final stage of the Euro 2008, Quaresma gave Scolari more reason to doubt him. Against the Czech Republic he played well, scored once and was well integrated in the team. Two days later, against Switzerland, he let everybody down again, playing individually, wasting opportunities with useless and pointless moves and avoiding any involvement in defence.

«It is one thing to play against a small team like Paços de Ferreira, and another to achieve a high standard of competition,» Luiz Felipe would like to point out, obviously with no offence intended towards smaller teams such as Paços de Ferreira.

When confronted with this subject, Scolari always answered that if it was a choice between Quaresma and Simão, he'd always choose the latter for his competitive maturity and knowledge, his tactical discipline and sense of team spirit. And during the last year of Luiz Felipe's reign as Portugal's manager, Quaresma still had to face the competition of Nani, who had developed a lot as a player since his move to Manchester United.

THE POWER OF WORDS
TEAM PREPARATION

Scolari has a very unusual way of approaching and preparing for matches. Even when it looks as if he's improvising (and it does happen occasionally) the truth is that most of his actions and words are prepared well in advance. At Portugal he would meet with Murtosa several times a day to analyse information, study tactics, anticipate the changes he might have to make during a match or in order to pre-empt an opponent's reactions.

He also likes to hold several individual and collective lectures. For these he brings along his files, videos and his instructions about the teams he is playing against. Scolari believes that the power of the word is fundamental in building a healthy relationship with his players and spreading his ideas effectively. For him, motivation is crucial and that is the process that leads the players to believe in him. Some of them have told me on many different occasions how emotive and inspiring his lectures are, and fundamental to overcoming psychological obstacles.

During periods when the players were away from home for a long time, such as Euro 2004 and 2008 or the 2006 World Cup, Scolari would frequently organise group lectures, normally in comfortable and private surroundings, to discuss his ideas about the other teams. Those were also the times when he stressed what he wanted from his players, giving them his instructions and motivating them.

One hour before each game, Scolari can't stand still, talking to each player, reminding them of their tasks, building up their egos. It's a period of great agitation. At half time, after a quick exchange of information with Murtosa and Samuel Pedroso, the FPF audio and sound manager, Luiz Felipe becomes more a therapist than a manager. Obviously, he reminds the players of the rights and wrongs of their performances but mainly he gives excited, lively and emotional talks in order to guide the players to what they are supposed to do.

During moments of crisis, of poor results, he holds meetings with the players asking *them* to talk, to contribute with ideas, good or bad. And the players, little by little, begin to open themselves up and to collaborate, allowing him to draw conclusions.

An example of Scolari's motivational drive was when he decided to screen some videos for his players that showed the extent of the support of the Portuguese people for their team. At the end of the Euro 2008 match against the Czech Republic, that led Portugal directly to the quarter-finals, in a live interview for the TV station TVI, he asked the station's CEO to provide him with a DVD containing images of people's reactions in Portugal and from around the world. He wanted to show them to the players so they could witness how important their victories were, the joy that they brought to every Portuguese person, so as to motivate his players and inculcate a sense of responsibility. Scolari also liked to bring to their attention some of the bad-mouthing of the team by some of their opponents as well as press and media comment which criticised them and disparaged the quality of the team.

Another mark that Scolari left on the Portuguese team was the way he always wanted the players to be relaxed before each game. The drive between the hotel and the stadium, when the work is done and there's nothing else to add, should be a time of joy and good spirits. The first surprise happened before the second game, against Brazil in the former Estádio das Antas. The goalkeeper Ricardo wrote in his book, *Diário de um Sonho*, that Scolari «values music as a way of relaxation and of stimulating the players. So he came up with the idea of asking the musician Roberto Leal for something to ease the tension there is before every match. Because Roberto is half Portuguese, half Brazilian, he asked for *Uma casa portuguesa, com certeza* (A Portuguese house without doubt), in a samba version. When the music started to play only two or three of us reacted. I started to clap, Pastilhas (Figo) got up and danced and Sérgio Conceição began yelling from the back. In the end, everybody partied and it was a fun trip. Funnily, Scolari didn't say much. He just wanted to see how we reacted.»

It was the first time that the team had ridden on that brand new bus, the windows of which allowed the privacy they needed. People on the outside couldn't see anything.

«It was really funny because people outside could never have imagined the party that was going on inside,» adds Ricardo.

Many of these methods had been successfully used by Scolari before, while he was working with the Brazilian team. A short passage from his diary, published in *Scolari, A Alma do Penta,* tells us of one particular episode:

«The players had already understood my 10 minute lecture and so I played a video about the Brazilian people with a song from Ivete Sangalo, with a typical '*baiano*' flavour. In it they could also see themselves scoring some really nice goals. It was very interesting to see their reaction. They've asked me to see the video again right before the game. I think we've accomplished our goal.»

On the morning of the 20th, after the defeat by Germany and the consequent elimination from Euro 2008, Scolari spoke to the players for the last time. He didn't want to say 'goodbye' instead he preferred to say 'thank you and see you around'. He described how grateful he was and went on to motivate the players in their careers. It was a brief speech, emotional and self-contained.

«I almost ended up crying,» he confessed to me.

Some of my friends who were there assured me that Scolari did indeed cry, but tried to hide it by pulling out a tissue to clean something that had got into his eye.

LEADING BY EXAMPLE
COSTINHA OUT

Before Euro 2004, in an interview that he gave to the European media, Scolari said:

«Costinha is a very valuable player for the Portuguese team. I know there are journalists who don't believe me but the truth is that a company doesn't only have one manager.»

Reality showed that, at the time, Costinha was an influential player in Mourinho's FC Porto and had always been one of Scolari's men. In spite of all the problems he had prior to the 2006 World Cup and his poor performances during that competition, Scolari still trusted him to help the team during the first qualification matches for Euro 2008. Even if his performances weren't great he needed a leader as Figo and Pauleta were out of the team. Things ran smoothly until the day Scolari felt that his trust had been shaken.

After winning against Azerbaijan 3-0, at the Estadio do Bessa, the home of Boavista Football Club, in Porto, and qualifying for Euro 2008, the players were entitled to their usual night out. But for some, the night extended until breakfast, even though a few players still had a training session the following morning at 10 o'clock. Portugal were playing in Poland four days later and the team still had a long flight to endure.

Scolari only found out what had happened the day of the match and was furious, even more so when he realised that the team's poor display would have to make him re-evaluate one of his principles: what the players do on their days off does not concern me. That now had to change because of the direct consequences on the pitch. Portugal lost in Chorzow, 2-1, and given the team's poor performance the result could have been considerably worse.

In this episode, Costinha was not the only one to have fully enjoyed the night out in a nightclub in Porto, but he was the team captain and for Scolari that made all the difference. For Scolari, Costinha should have set the standard, led by example. He should have been the first one to tell his team mates that it was late and that they all still had a long journey and a very difficult game ahead of them in four days time. Obviously, Scolari never raised this in public when he was questioned about Costinha and Maniche's removal from the team. Actually, as he has always said from his very first day, he doesn't like to explain his team selections. And he never will.

And just as had happened during the six months prior to Euro 2004, when he was also out of the Portuguese team, Maniche accepted the fact quietly, without publicly questioning Scolari's decision. And perhaps this is the reason why, a year later, he was called up again to join his team mates – unlike Costinha, who never was. When Scolari realises that the players have taken advantage of the freedom that he gives them, he doesn't hesitate to impose stricter rules. As he did when he decided to ban alcohol on the team's charter flights, a ban that also affected everybody else on the plane, including friends and family. One day, coming back from Kuwait, some of the players had had too much to drink and so Scolari felt it was time to cut out the alcohol totally and impose a 'dry regime'.

Wine with meals, though, is not forbidden, except on match days. This was not something that Scolari set up but rather something that he happily accepted, seeing it as an adjustment to the Portuguese way of life. Before him, Humberto Coelho and António Oliveira had already given the players permission to have a glass of wine at each meal. They'd preferred to accept that situation rather than watch players trying to trick them by putting wine in a coloured plastic cup or in a bottle of dark coloured juice.

*I'm not interested
in suing. I like to sort
things out my
own way.*

THE PUNCH
THE TOUGHEST MOMENT

It was Friday, September 14, 4 o'clock in the afternoon – less than 48 hours after Scolari had punched the Serbian player Ivica Dragutinovic. The news on the internet said something about the referee's report. Apparently the observer's report had come down on the side of Luiz Felipe and that was a positive sign. I later learned that the report made by the Portugal-Serbia match referee also pointed in the same direction, even stating that Scolari had been provoked.

I called Luiz Felipe, for the fourth time in two days. He was out walking, something he often did, with Murtosa and their wives, Olga and Lisete, on the *'calçadão'* by Boca do Inferno, in the area between Cascais and Guincho.

The landscape is of immense beauty but the voice I heard was sadder than ever. All of a sudden, I could almost see him jump for joy at the other end of the phone as I told him about the referee's report. He asked me if I was joking and I listened to him as he gave the good news to Olga, Murtosa and Lisete.

«Zé, that's wonderful, I really needed to hear that. Did the referee actually write that? I can't believe it... He'd hurt us before several times and now he writes I was not to blame entirely? That's wonderful!»

When we said goodbye I felt Luiz Felipe was greatly relieved.

The night of the match, Scolari didn't have the courage to face Olga when he got home, his friend and wife for forty years. His boys also criticised him although they understood that those things happen in football. But Olga was harsh:

«Felipe, you should be ashamed of yourself. You have closed the doors to a career in Europe. You shouldn't have done it! You shouldn't have!»

Olga repeated this several times to an ashamed Luiz Felipe, whose only words were to ask for forgiveness from his wife and children.

«It was the worst day of my life,» he confessed to me days later.

Could Luiz Felipe have calmed down the whole situation, on the night of the game, during the press conference? Of course, he could have. I was at home watching the game on TV and when it happened, I turned to my wife and said:

«The guy is lost. Someone's got to help him. He has to apologise immediately.»

I grabbed the phone to try and get hold of some of the people from the Portuguese delegation but no one answered because of the confusion that had resulted. I was informed later that some people had tried to calm him down. One of them was Luís Figo, who had flown to Lisbon to support his ex-team mates and friends on such an important game for the Portuguese team. Figo talked with Scolari and asked him to calm down and to make a public apology.

Scolari arrived at the press conference in better spirits, more calm and relaxed, but he lost his temper again and changed his mind about what he had initially planned to do. Was it because the TV images were inconclusive? I had my doubts but after watching the press conference I was convinced that Scolari had not been in the right frame of mind to do it. If I had been in charge of conducting this affair then Scolari wouldn't have given RTP (the Portuguese public broadcasting corporation) the interview or gone to the press conference after the game. Someone else could have done it for him, probably Murtosa, and

Murtosa could have given the first indication of an apology. Knowing Luiz Felipe's personality, his reaction was inevitable in such a volatile and hostile environment. Still, at least he stated that he hadn't punched the Serbian and he apologised to Portugal.

Scolari is a very religious man. He's a catholic, a faith that comes from his family. His mother, Dona Leida, was a committed catholic who wouldn't allow her children to go to the cinema unless they had gone to church first.

In his book, *Diário de um Sonho*, Ricardo wrote that moments before the Euro 2004 debut game, when the team had got back to the changing rooms after the usual pre-game warm-up, the manager called the whole group together. They joined hands and prayed together. The goalkeeper described it as «a magical moment».

Over the years, Scolari became a true devoté to Nossa Senhora do Caravaggio (Our Lady of Caravaggio) and frequently, as a true pilgrim, he visits her altar in Ferroupilha, in Rio Grande do Sul. He always keeps two images on his lockers: Nossa Senhora de Caravaggio and Fátima.

I'm convinced that, at that moment, when everything was going so badly for him, when things were, apparently, falling apart, he might have felt that he had lost the help that he had been counting on for years. It's a thought that goes through every true believer's mind a million times: if things are not working out, if life turns hellish, then it's divine intervention. Whoever looks after us is no longer doing so.

I later became aware as to why Scolari hadn't been given any information about the content of the TV images. As usual, the audiovisual manager at the FPF, Samuel Pedroso, had recorded the images directly onto his laptop – which allows, amongst other things, an almost instant statistical analysis – from the satellite signal provided by RTP.

As soon as the game had ended, and because it was felt that the Serbian goal shouldn't have been a goal, Samuel stopped recording and went to see Scolari in the changing room so that he could see the footage immediately. What happened therefore was that the incidents after the game were not captured and no one saw the images in real time. And so, when Scolari went to the press conference, neither he nor any of his colleagues knew about it. The day after, bearing in mind the hard reality, there was a meeting with Scolari's closest colleagues, held in the house of one of the members of staff, to plan his defence strategy. He gave a public apology and an interview to RTP that was intended to reinforce the idea that he never walked away from protecting his players and defending his team.

In the days that followed the 'punching episode' things became even more heated because of José Mourinho's sudden departure from Chelsea. Immediately, rumours spread that the FPF was ready to hire Mourinho and let Scolari go. At the time, under UEFA rules, there could have been a four match ban – which was the number of games the team still needed to qualify.

But it was Mourinho himself who brought the speculation to an end by making a statement, in London, that he was not ready, at that moment in his career, to work with the national team. He added that Portugal were in good hands.

These words may come as some surprise knowing the coldness of the relationship that they've always had, but there's more to this matter that might be worth telling.

In April 2007, when invited to visit the Shimon Perez Centre for Peace, in Israel, Scolari was greeted and looked after by Avram Grant, the manager who, later, took Mourinho's place. Luiz Felipe knew that Grant was a key person in the Roman Abramovich regime. So, when the Israeli started to ask him questions – which players he'd choose if he was Chelsea's manager, if he would be available, when would he be free from the contract with the FPF, etc. – Scolari cut to the chase and told Avram Grant that he was not interested in the position adding that he felt that Chelsea were already in very good hands.

Once in Lisbon, Scolari passed this message on to Mourinho, through his manager Jorge Mendes. Mourinho was grateful and later returned the gesture publicly.

Should Scolari have been fired because of the Dragutinovic incident? If he had been, surely his critics would have approved and Scolari's enemies would have rejoiced. Even I would have accepted it and I'm certainly neither a critic or an enemy. And I let Luiz Felipe know this at the time during a conversation in which I reprimanded him, like a younger brother.

There were two main reasons that he didn't get fired: firstly, the day that the opportunity arose, Mourinho wasn't available, and secondly, there was concern that replacing Scolari at that moment for someone other than Mourinho could have been the end of all the hard development work of the previous four years. The officials at the FPF, from its president Gilberto Madaíl down, knew that it was a risk not worth taking, as some of the players could even have refused to play for the Portuguese team. In the end, the FPF saved the day. After the matches against Azerbaijan and Kazakhstan Scolari was fined 35,000 Euros – money that was used to start a Fair-Play fund.

Strangely, the amount of that fine was one of the reasons for the cooling of the relationship between Scolari and Madaíl, as it was three times more than the amount that UEFA usually imposed in similar situations.

Speaking of fines, I can now reveal that there were clauses in Scolari's contract with the FPF which related to compensation, one of which detailed what each had to pay to the other in the event of an early termination of the contract. If the FPF were to have fired Scolari, he would have received 300,000 Euros. If it had been the other way around, then Scolari would have had to pay the FPF 3,000,000 Euros!

LECTURES AND LEADERSHIP
FOOTBALL & THE CORPORATE WORLD

Scolari is an excellent communicator and that, I believe, is one of the secrets of his success as a manager. But unlike some other managers I've seen – who are also good communicators in their work environment – Scolari is also very much at ease when talking in public to many varied audiences.

I've accompanied him to several lectures outside the football world and I've realised that he is able to take advantage of the many facets of his personality in a way that very few people can. Most of the lectures are about team building. The audiences want to hear him talking about the similarities between winning in football and winning in the corporate environment. Scolari recounts some of his experiences, episodes in his life, and unusual stories to illustrate his points and to engage the audience.

It seemed to me that he never felt out of place no matter who the audience were in front of him. He always seemed at ease. I have frequently heard him apologising for «always talking about the same thing, which is football», but inevitably the examples that he uses fit like a glove in terms of the leadership points that he wants to stress and, consequently, he always meets the expectations of both his audience and the event organisers.

Scolari made good money from these lectures. Actually, the ability to accept invitations such as these was part of his contract with the FPF. He also insisted on complete independence in managing any advertising deals he was involved in. That was the only way he stayed the national manager for five years. His salary, although double the amount that had been paid to his predecessors, António Oliveira or Humberto Coelho, represented just a quarter of his total income.

During those presentations with their very varied audiences – college students, corporate managers, sales reps – Scolari discovered something very important for his own career in Portugal: people liked him, even when things didn't look good for him either because of poor results or because of negative actions on his part.

For example, a week after the Portugal-Serbia match, at which the incident with Dragutinovic had taken place, Scolari was scheduled to give a lecture to a private company. After he'd pulled himself together after the incident he still felt that he should cancel the lecture as he wasn't feeling psychologically strong enough to face the public... especially as the event was taking place in the city of Porto. Four managers from the company, a multi-national operating in the food industry, went to the FPF's headquarters and told him:

«Don't even think of pulling out. We don't care about what happened in the match.»

After their continued insistence, Scolari finally gave in. And during the lecture, in a very clever way, he introduced the Dragutinovic incident as an example of what not to do in the process of motivating colleagues. After an hour and a half, much to his amazement, he received a standing ovation from the audience of 300 people. With eyes watering, he thanked them.

THE NEW CAPTAINS
VETERANS ABANDONED

Managing a football team is not an easy task, especially when it includes a lot of top players, some of them still in the process of maturing. It's even harder when a good number of these athletes only have a basic education, a rudimentary one – people who have put aside the reading of a book in preference to kicking a ball so as to follow their own dreams or the aspirations of their parents.

When arriving in Portugal, Scolari only knew about half a dozen players, but he quickly understood that this mixed group comprised both first rate players and third rate ones, as well as those who were vain and preferred to bask in the limelight and those who preferred to stay in the background. And then there were those who could scarcely disguise their envy of a colleague's success.

Dealing with such a group was not a problem for him, not only because of his extensive experience – let's not forget he had managed the World Champion team, a team in which vanities are stronger than in any other European one – but also because he knew how to take advantage of the natural leadership qualities he found in players such as Fernando Couto, captain at the time, or Luís Figo or Pedro Pauleta – his three pillars of strength.

Fernando Couto has always been a strong leader, someone who has always imposed himself through a positive, very professional and calm attitude, very different to the 'Karate Kid' idea many people in Portugal had of him. He was the only player who would sit at the top of the table and none of his team mates would leave it without asking his permission. He always wanted to know how the press conferences were going for his team mates, and if they were being pressured by the press he always showed solidarity with them.

Luís Figo was a different type of leader, who knew how to choose the right words, persuading his team mates and leading by example. But he also knew that he was one of the best players in the World – FIFA gave him that distinction in 2001 – and that fact alone was enough to place him first amongst the other players.

Sometimes – to put an end to any small incident – all he needed to do was to give a look – that cold look of a strong face, with no sign of a smile. But he was also a joker, almost like a child having fun away from the rollercoaster of fame.

Pedro Pauleta needed more time to come out as a leader and he is one of those who doesn't hide the fact that Scolari was the manager who helped and valued him the most. He was the team's 'ugly duckling' as he didn't have a background in any of the young national teams nor had he played with any of the big Portuguese clubs. He almost missed out by being sent off in the first half of a Euro 2000 match. But Pauleta was an unquestionable professional, with extraordinary levels of concentration and commitment. An honest man of great integrity, he was not afraid to give his opinion even if it was against the status quo. Between 2004 and 2006, as a result of his natural talent, he was very much the 'conductor' of the team.

Fernando Couto was the captain when Scolari arrived and he held on to the position until he was substituted in the Euro 2004 debut game against Greece. Luiz Felipe was thinking of handing the honour of captain to Figo but his respect for Couto's past persuaded him to wait.

Figo was, to Scolari, the true team leader and the natural

captain. And for more than one reason: he was the most renowned and respected man in the team, feared by their opponents and by referees.

When Euro 2008 arrived, Scolari had a leadership problem to solve. Cristiano Ronaldo was undoubtedly the most feared player in everybody's eyes but within the group he was not really seen as a captain and he was also an easy focus for envy, something that some players could not hide.

A hero of the 'Golden Generation', Nuno Gomes was Scolari's last captain. A somewhat discreet but self-assured captain, he was committed and demanding of his fellow team mates. He managed to be the bridge between the older players and the 'new tigers' who were looking to confirm their status. But, nevertheless, Nuno Gomes was no Figo or Pauleta and Scolari dealt with this matter in the sort of way that King Solomon might have – as he had done when he had lost the midfielder Émerson, his team captain in the Brazilian team, on the eve of the 2002 World Cup. He nominated five leaders, putting an end to some of the rivalries and finding a balance between several of the cliques within the group. Besides Nuno Gomes, the players that he nominated were Cristiano Ronaldo, Petit, Ricardo Carvalho and Simão Sabrosa. During Euro 2008, whenever Nuno Gomes was substituted, the captain's armband was to be handed over to Cristiano Ronaldo.

*South American coaches,
especially Brazilians
and Argentinians, have a
certain mystique about them.
We make everything enjoyable,
and that's what football's
all about – having fun!*

QUIM WASN'T CHOSEN
RICARDO ALWAYS WAS

Ricardo was one of the most notable cases of how Scolari can motivate players. Although he'd always been the manager's first choice, the confidence that Scolari had shown in him was never reflected outside the group and he continued to have numerous critics. The way he reacted to some of the things that were said about him or about his performance suggested an insecure player. Nevertheless, his qualities as goalkeeper are very clear, especially between the posts. His sense of position and his excellent reflex response to short distance strikes provided some memorable performances.

Ricardo has always been one of the hardest working players during the training sessions, exchanging information with Quim and with Brassard, the goalkeeping coach. He would always study videos showing how the opponent's strikers operated and this paid off, especially during the penalty kicks against England (In Euro 2004 and the 2006 World Cup).

In Lisbon, in Estádio da Luz, it was a very intense and balanced match, with Portugal managing to bring the match to 1-1 (in the 82nd minute) and England managing to pull it back to 2-2 in the second half of extra time. When extra time finished they moved on to penalties – the match was still very much in the balance.

It was after the sixth shot that Ricardo was inspired: he removed his gloves and kept out Darius Vassel's strike. And then, he asked Scolari to let him take the penalty for Portugal, instead of Nuno Valente, who had been originally chosen.

Ricardo's determination couldn't have been stronger. From a distance he signalled to Scolari, with gestures that suggested that they'd agreed to it before. The truth is that when he was preparing to take the kick he didn't even look at the goalkeeper David James. It was as if he just saw an empty goal. He scored, taking Portugal into the quarter-finals.

Two years later, on the stage of the magnificent Gelsenkirchen stadium, it was a new game and a new set of penalty kicks. But this time, it was an even bigger drama. The night before Ricardo had spent most of his time studying the English way of taking penalties. He watched the videos for hours but, of course, nothing was guaranteed. What happened next is World Cup history.

Ricardo ended up being the first goalkeeper ever to keep out three penalty kicks during the penalty shoot out, leaving the England team devastated. During those long minutes of standing there, the solitary hero, with most of the English supporters behind him, found a particular source of inspiration, as he later told the reporters:

«I discovered, amongst the English supporters, a Portuguese one. A short guy, by himself, with a scarf and a flag, standing amongst the opposition. I kept looking at him while I was waiting for my turn to defend and he became my connection with the Portuguese people. But defending the penalties was also a matter of work, study and motivation. I knew the English team might be hesitant if they recalled what had happened two years before and that's exactly what did happen. After the first penalty shot I felt we were going to win.»

When Euro 2008 arrived, Ricardo's critics were more vociferous than ever as he had not had a very good season with Real Bétis. In comparison Quim had been very succesful at Benfica. But I knew Luiz Felipe was not going to drop Ricardo.

Actually, the conversation that we had, during a workshop for the Euro team, at which José Manuel Freitas from *A Bola* was also present, dissipated any doubts that I might have had.

Luiz Felipe was not happy with the way in which we presented him with the pros and cons for each of the goalkeepers. Scolari, with his trained eye for the details that we could not possibly see, convinced us of one thing: Ricardo was staying. The manager valued Ricardo's abilities between the posts and compared him to Quim:

«I don't trust him if it's a low ball coming from left side. Our opponents may have observed the same and that's not good for the team.»

On the eve of the debut game, against Turkey, bad luck knocked at Quim's door. He got injured at the last minute in training and had to be replaced by Nuno Espírito Santo. Quim's expectation of being the Portuguese goalkeeper was higher than ever, and so it was a massive disappointment.

«I felt this was the biggest chance I had to be Portugal's goalkeeper,» Quim explained the day after his injury, «but life goes on and I just hope that Portugal can be European Champions,» he concluded, in his usual straightforward manner.

What happened at Euro 2008 served to remind me, José Manuel Freitas, and many other journalists, of the doubts that we had about Ricardo's ability to deal with pressure.

Against Germany and the Czech Republic he let in goals that were struck from within the box, giving everybody the sense that he could have done more than just leap at them with his eyes closed and then make gestures towards his team mates. At that moment, while I was talking with some of my colleagues, I was reminded of something that Agostinho Oliveira had told me, many years before:

«Quim is as good as the best players, especially because he

has a very strong psychological side to his charcter. He's spent most of his career with a minor club where he got used to hard work, and to letting in goals. He can move on without bothering what people have to say. Unlike some others.»

Nothing can guarantee that things would have been different if Quim had not been injured as Scolari's choice had already been made. The same Ricardo who had saved Portugal twice against England, had an equally decisive role, negatively speaking, in the premature end of the Portuguese adventure at Euro 2008. For him, one could say he managed to remain as Scolari's firt choice right until the very end. Literally.

THE ART OF WAR
THE INSPIRATION OF BOOKS

As a leader, Scolari is frequently inspired by various quotes and texts, by simple stories or even fables which he uses to get his message across. During Euro 2004, he returned to his favourite of many years, *The Art of War*, by Sun Tzu – a text he used to support the players psychologically. And during the campaign for the 2006 World Cup, he used *Voando como uma águia*, (Flying like an eagle) by João Roberto Gretz, a renowned Brazilian speaker.

For the opening game of the 2008 World Cup, against Turkey, he once again decided to use *The Art of War*. A justifiable choice given the fact that, on one hand, half of the players were working with him for the first time and, on the other, it was a critical match if Portuguese aspirations were to be met.

For many of the players, the Czech Republic were the best team, in terms of technique. At the physical level they were also very convincing. But for Scolari, the Turkish team were also very committed to the game, with great individual skills and a huge spirit when it came to overcoming adversity, something which became very apparent as the competition progressed. They had to be respected and dealt with responsibly. A victory over Turkey would be a huge step towards qualifying which is the reason that Scolari insisted on the psychological preparation as well as the usual study of the technical side and of tactics.

Once he was free from his contract as the Portugal manager, Scolari provided me with some of the material that he used in preparing for that game. It's an incisive text full of sub-texts and direct appeals.

Sun-Tzu's thoughts alert us to the everyday challenges. We live in the era of knowledge. Knowledge is the main resource and richness in our modern society. Everybody knows that. What we have to add to that is that knowledge without a practical side has no meaning. This is the reason why we need to believe in the value of work and knowledge. The intensity of every moment should give us the stamina to take the next step towards victory. Our path should be as enjoyable as our destination. But for that, we need to believe. Believe. In your dreams. Believe. In your talent. In your possibilities. In your abilities. Believe. In your family, in your friends, in your team mates, in your fellow compatriots, because they expect a lot from you. Believe. In challenges. In difficulties. In the possibility of a dark day. Believe. To hesitate is to stop. Not fighting is to stop. Believe. In every moment. In good ones and all others. By believing, the World and its Creator will work with us to our benefit.

BELIEVE.
IF YOU WANT IT,
YOU AND EVERY ONE OF US,
WE CAN.

A good day to all of you.
Count on me. I know I can count on you.

The result of the Portugal-Turkey match was a win for Portugal by 2-0 and, above all, a beautiful display by the Portuguese team, a demonstration of the group's individual and collective qualities, a constant overcoming of the difficulties that were created by the Turkish – a key team in the path of Portugal.

For the next game, against the Czech Republic, Scolari did a similar thing, although he used different texts. The result was another win, this time 3-1. A victory that led Portugal through to the quarter-finals.

After the group stage had finished, Scolari still had to find ways to keep the players inspired, to keep the flame alive, to reinforce their concentration and to ask them to give more than they had ever thought possible.

After joking at the press conference about the different heights of the Portuguese and the German players, Scolari softened his language to appeal to his own players and to their emotions. He began with a quote from the filmmaker Frederico Fellini:

«There's no beginning, there's no end. Just an infinite passion for life.»

And then in a two page document, the manager searched for the players' souls.

In our life, work, and family, and in all the places we're in, we need to be ready to learn lessons. The world is our teacher. Our mission in life is not to change the world. Our mission is to change ourselves. We're moving on in our journey thanks to everyone's commitment to the group. The truth about our team is based on the following values: we're a unique group because we have a common dream and we're united around it. We have a cause. We're articulate people and we have the ability to establish and sustain our relationship with enthusiasm, whether we play or not. We're humble. We demonstrate mutual respect. We're transparent. We always search for the best result. We know our responsibilities. We cultivate good humour at all times. We have arrived here because of the important contribution of each of you. We want to go further. To go further means to face new challenges. New and bigger challenges because every time we go one step further there's a new landscape to work on, with its details and risks. Our next step follows the first one. The opportunity the world gives us every day: the first step is to sow the seed. As wisdom tells us, if we sow thoughts we reap our actions. By sowing our actions, we reap our habits. By sowing our habits, we reap our personality. By sowing our personality, we reap our destiny. And our destiny, and our thoughts, our actions, all our habits and our personality will lead us to the victory, for all of us!

A GOOD NEW JOURNEY!

Count on me. I know I can count on you.

In these texts Scolari never mentions the opponent's name. That's a conscious decision. His priority is to appeal to his men, to their qualities, asking them to overcome themselves. There is no need to 'individualise' the enemy. As Luiz Felipe would say:

«The worst enemy is the one inside us, when we doubt, when we don't believe in ourselves and in our collective and individual capabilities.»

In Portugal, Scolari also used an original formula to give the players something on which they could reflect. Under the door of each of their hotel rooms he would slip a story or a fable with a conclusion that served the motivational needs of a given game. The day after, he would encourage group discussion about it, to try to ensure that the message was more effectively passed on.

He first introduced this method while he was working as Brazil's manager. In the book, *Scolari, a alma do Penta*, the author writes that, before the match with China, the easiest opponent in the group, and with Brazil already qualified for the next stage of the competition, Scolari himself slipped a piece of paper under each door on which was written the following story:

A lion hunter invited two friends to go hunting with him and as a precaution asked a sorcerer for a magic flute: he only needed to blow the flute and the lion would start to dance and stopped chasing them. This meant that they could catch him and kill him, without any risk. And that's what happened with the first lion they encountered. Up in a tree, a monkey was watching what was going on, silently. With the second lion, the same thing happened. The flute was really working well and the monkey was still watching, silently. When it came to the third lion the flute didn't work. And so the hunters were eaten up by the lion. That's when the monkey said: "I was just waiting to see when they would come across a deaf lion...»

In a subliminal way, the manager put across several messages. The most important was that one cannot trust too much or relax even when winning. One can never underestimate an opponent. The Chinese team, although apparently easy and fragile, could always have turned out to be the deaf lion.

CHELSEA HERE I COME
MADAÍL ALREADY KNEW

Like most managers and players, Scolari does not negotiate, in person, all the details of his contracts. After discussing the basic guidelines of what he wants and doesn't want to be safeguarded in the formal agreement, he allows most details to be resolved by the people who represent him, mainly Gilmar Veloz. There's a third stage, even before putting his signature on the contract, during which he analyses it once more, asks for explanations, explores any areas of doubt, leaving no loose ends that might lead to later misunderstandings.

Scolari is one of those people for whom his 'word' is enough to tie up an agreement. Even if he has to discuss it later, to fill out more of the detail, even if he has to back down on this or that point, once his word has been given there is no going back.

It was the word he gave to Madaíl that led to him being granted three contracts with the FPF. The details came later and not always in line with what he had expected. The first contract, negotiated in November and December 2002, was the most complex one as it included some matters not only about himself but also about his direct collaborators, his colleagues who had accompanied him from Brazil: Flávio Teixeira (Murtosa) and Darlan Schneider. Details such as the house, the car, trips to Brazil, forms of payment, image rights, etc. all had to be sorted out for the first time.

In June 2004, after having made the gesture of putting the ring on his finger at the famous press conference after the Portugal-Holland match at Euro 2004, Scolari and the FPF redefined some of the detail that had been contained in the previous agreement, mainly a salary rise and a greater autonomy when it came to advertising deals.

The third contract, in June 2006, was the one that least pleased Scolari. Not for financial reasons but because Madaíl wouldn't contemplate extending the term of the contract, that was due to end in June, until after Euro 2008, in which Portugal were supposed to be competing, and did.

When, on 10 July 2006, he heard Dona Olga's *No* to the CBF offer that had been made to him by its president Ricardo Teixeira, Scolari returned to the negotiation table. Madaíl awaited him anxiously.

«President,» Luiz Felipe said, «I'm staying. It's in your hands to determine how long I'm staying, although I think it would be good for the team's growth that we sign a four year contract, given the World Cup in 2010. If you want, I will sign right now and we can close the matter.»

Madaíl refused. Later, he said it was never his intention to agree to contracts with dates beyond his own personal mandate or the competitive cycle.

Actually, it wasn't always quite like that. António Oliveira – who had left Madaíl only three months after he was made the FPF's president for the first time, in 1996, and had exchanged his position as manager of the Portuguese team for that of FC Porto manager during Euro 96. He had a two year contract at the beginning of the campaign for the World Cup 2002 that was, later, extended to 2004, some say against Madaíl's wish. After the Korea-Japan World Cup, the FPF fired António Oliveira and had to pay him a huge sum in compensation.

Luiz Felipe confided to me, that same month of July, that by insisting on a two year contract, Madaíl was «opening the door to a mandatory end of the relationship after Euro 2008. Are we going back to the same thing? I will have to prove, once again, that I'm worth it? If the work is good, if I get along very well with the players, if we agree we need to keep making changes, include younger players, prepare for the future, why are we going to repeat a process which is so tiring for everybody?»

When Chelsea tried to hire Scolari, even before Euro 2008, Scolari wanted to leave the FPF, which is not to say that he wanted to leave the team.

«Working with the players is never tiring,» he told me so many times «what's hard is the behind the scenes work....»

Inside the FPF, Scolari always counted on the full support and professional commitment of the human and logistic operation led by Carlos Godinho. His weariness came from the relationship with the FPF's officials, especially Gilberto Madaíl.

For years, Scolari and Madaíl were in harmony, praising one another in pubic and being very supportive of each other. But at several key moments, Scolari felt that Madaíl could have been more incisive in his defence of the team manager, especially in response to those critics and to those episodes that were coming from the usual places, such as FC Porto and from some of the anti-Scolari commentators.

On his side, Scolari always tried to present a conciliatory image of their relationship. Perhaps the most notable case was the one that occurred in Basel, when he was asked for the first time about his leaving for Chelsea. Without ever saying the club's name, Scolari mentioned he'd had a very tempting offer of work, and that the financial terms were also very attractive. He also said that he was waiting for Madaíl's final word, as he was looking for assistance from some investors. He let this be known even though he didn't have to. But the truth was that Madaíl had known for a long time that Scolari wanted to leave and he didn't make any effort to keep him. To be precise, when the Portugal team first gathered in Viseu, before Euro 2008, Madaíl already knew that he would have to look for another manager right after the competition. He'd got only himself to blame for dragging the case out longer than was necessary.

It's a nonsense to say that Chelsea's announcement that they had secured Scolari affected the players, or that it destabilised the environment and was responsible for the poor result against Switzerland. We should look at the Spanish example. The manager, Luiz Aragonés, also announced that he would be leaving the team to work with Fenerbahçe, in Turkey. This was announced between the second and third matches of the group stage. And that fact didn't stop the Spanish team from going on to win the competition in an entirely deserved way.

We shouldn't be naïve. Who, in the modern society in which we live, with all the technology that is now available, didn't already know how close Scolari and Chelsea were? Even the players knew that Scolari was leaving for Chelsea. Deco, for instance, completely put aside in Barcelona, refused an offer from Inter Milan so that he could join him at Chelsea. It's clear that the announcement was not a surprise to the players though people liked to suggest that it was.

The only reason why the timing was not good seems more to do with it being an affirmation of the power and money of Roman Abramovich. The club had received the final yes from Scolari two weeks before and could easily have waited another week before revealing to the world the name of their new manager. But the London club opted not to, and when Scolari knew of its intentions he talked with Madaíl and they both agreed that the situation was out of their control.

When approaching Scolari, Chelsea opted for a different strategy to the one that the FA had adopted two years before. The first contacts were discreet, although they had actually started even before the Champions League Final. It wouldn't have mattered whether or not Avram Grant had won – something Mourinho hadn't achieved in his three years – he would still have left. Roman Abramovich wanted to replace him with Scolari.

At an advanced stage of the contacts – Scolari always kept in communication with the FPF and Gilberto Madaíl – he asked for a period of time to concentrate on the Portuguese team's work. It was in Viseu, during the pre-competition training, that the pre-agreement was settled. The morning of May 31, hours before flying to Switzerland, Scolari met with Chelsea representatives.

They gave him an ultimatum. There were only two options: himself or Lippi. But they preferred him. They needed an answer in a week.

It was Peter Kenyon, Chelsea's Chief Executive, who told him. It appeared that Roman Abramovich had said that he wouldn't take no for an answer this time. The previous April, when Chelsea had made their first approach, Abramovich had understood Scolari's reasons but now he felt he had no reason to say no. It took Scolari only a minute to give an answer:

«I accept. I'm going to Chelsea.»

He had given his word.

A week later, once the details had been clarified, he put his signature down on paper.

It's a surprise for me that people say Chelsea are unpopular, because when we went to China, they cry for Chelsea, they love Chelsea...

A BITTER FAREWELL
LOSING AGAINST GERMANY

«My God, what a disappointment...I didn't sleep at all last night. I never thought we would end this way, losing a game we were supposed to win...Mistakes? Zé, forget it. I don't want to blame anyone. It's not worth it. We lost, it's all over.»

I had this conversation with Luiz Felipe Scolari the morning after the defeat against Germany, it was barely 11 o'clock. A few minutes later, Madaíl would be talking with the press about Scolari's departure for Chelsea. I couldn't resist asking Scolari:

«Felipe, have you given any indication about the future manager for Portugal?»

He already had his answer:

«No I haven't, nor will I, even if they ask me. I don't want to be linked with this process because I don't want people to say the president only does what I tell him to. That's his decision alone.»

The disappointing evening after the 2-3 defeat by Germany in the Euro 2008 quarter-finals was spent with his closest colleagues: Murtosa, Darlan, Brassard and, of course, Carlos Godinho. They enjoyed a few hours together that were very cathartic, reviewing their years of work together, work that had come to an end two weeks earlier than they felt it should have. They also discussed what had gone wrong in the match, the avoidable mistakes, the options they had had, the choices they had made – all of which could no longer be corrected.

The sun was rising behind the Neuchâtel Lake when they went back to their rooms. Alone, Scolari prayed to the images of

Nossa Senhora do Caravaggio and Fátima, then lay down and tried to sleep. He got up less than an hour later unable to close his eyes or to forget his sad farewell to the Portuguese team.

He felt that the whole world would be pointing the finger of blame at him for his blind trust in Ricardo, for putting Paulo Ferreira on the left side of defence, leaving Caneira out of his chosen 23 players, or for the total lack of coordination that the Portuguese defence had shown during the match with Germany. But more than ever, Scolari was not worried about the critics. His only goal was to get to the end of each match and ask himself the question: «Did you do everything you could have done?»

That evening, the answer was a clear *Yes*.

During the two months prior to Euro 2008, Scolari had lived through his worst period of doubt since taking on the position of manager. In February, he had revealed his fears:

«We don't have midfield players, everybody is injured. We don't have Deco, we don't have Petit, Tiago is not playing for months... If things go on like this, I don't know what do.»

He also confessed how disappointed he had been by the lack of competitive spirit that he had seen from some of the players in the friendly match against Italy, in Zurich. Yet at the same time, a month later, after the test against Greece, he also expressed to me his satisfaction with the performances of Nuno Gomes and Hugo Almeidas. During this complicated selection period, Scolari hesitated more than ever. And to complicate the situation even more, he had to face instability within the team following the announcement by the FPF of the amount of the bonus payments that the players would receive for each of the matches in the competition.

As usual there were performance awards, the largest that had ever been paid out so far. And as always, when it comes to money, problems emerge. Some of the players started to raise various niggles and complaints about small details – even about things that amounted to less than 200 euros a day. Scolari had no hesitation: he wasn't risking the unity of the team or the team spirit, even if it meant that he would have to drop some of the most valued players.

As I noted in *Record* at the time, whilst I know which players were involved I don't intend to mention them by name. And although I understand Scolari's decision, I didn't quite agree with it. But the truth of the matter is – in this case as in so many others – Scolari makes his own decisions and, true to form, he always refuses to comment on the players that he doesn't select.

Unlike the 2006 World Cup, I didn't take the risk (in *Record*) of presenting my final list of the 23 players that I believed would be selected for the European competition held in Switzerland and Austria. The manager's own doubts were more than enough for me to avoid such an unnecessary risk. Still, I had to come up with a list of probable players, just as every other journalist does who follows the progress of the Portuguese team. As was proved on the day that Scolari's own squad list became public, it was very different to that of the journalists.

The day that he arrived at his small room in Solar do Dão, in Viseu, May 12, Luiz Felipe watched me as I pulled a funny face at him. I had just realised that at least one of the names I had written in *Record* that very same day was wrong. Like all the other reporters, I had decided to include Maniche's name, but instead Scolari had picked his brother, Jorge Ribeiro. It was my fault for not understanding the clues that Luiz Felipe had given me the week before:

«If you have doubts about A does that mean you'll choose B?» I had asked him.

«Maybe, but Jorge Ribeiro can also play in that position,» he had answered.

«But in the midfield, player X could be a good alternative to player Y,» I insisted.

«Yes but Jorger Ribeiro is also an option,» he replied.

Scolari mentioned his name not twice but three times before he revealed the final list.

Maniche's absence was a surprise to me and to many other observers. Still, Scolari's decision was only because of the few appearances that Maniche had made during the previous months – something that may seem contradictory when you consider that Petit, for example, had not been playing for more than two months because of injury. But for Scolari, Maniche was not the same player that he had been in May 2006, a time when Luiz Felipe had trusted him even after a bad season with Dynamo Moscow and Chelsea. In May 2008, Maniche had played less than 10 games out of a possible 25 for Inter Milan and his tremendous physical attributes seemed to have diminished.

As a replacement for Maniche, Scolari chose João Moutinho who, although he had very different qualities, was turning out positive performances, always above average. Two years before, during the World Cup in Germany, Scolari had hesitated and had ended up leaving him out of the competition, putting him in the Under-21 team instead, a team which played in the European competition in Portugal. But now, Luiz Felipe had no doubts. Moutinho was one of his strongest bets and the player confirmed, during the competition, that the manager was right.

Maniche's reaction left the manager very disappointed. He accused Scolari of being influenced in his decision to leave him out, suggesting that Carlos Godinho might have been the one responsible.

«People like to say they've helped me on this and that occasion but they forget I helped them many times too,» Luiz Felipe told me, without mentioning Maniche or any other player.

Carlos Godinho couldn't have been angrier about the way that his name was being linked to this controversy. When we were in Viseu, Godinho told me:

«Like millions of other Portuguese I can't forget Maniche's brilliant displays in Euro 2004 and the 2006 World Cup. I may have been surprised by his absence at Euro 2008, but accusing me of influencing the manager? This manager, of all people, who has never been influenced by anyone outside of his own coaching staff? The person who said that, obviously, doesn't know me or Scolari and the way he works.»

I'd like to take a moment to acknowledge Carlos Godinho's work as Director of Football at the FPF. He is the man in the organisation who works closest with the national team manager. He's always been a major help to each of them and they have all praised his work – Humberto Coelho, António Oliveira (at least while he was still on speaking terms with Godinho and the FPF...) and Scolari, and all of those prior to them. Godinho's competence in all matters related to organising a top level football team was at such a high level that when Scolari was invited to be Benfica's manager he thought about inviting him to be a part of his team.

Scolari was the same manager when he started the campaign for Euro 2008, with the same ambitions, but in his mind he knew that his options were limited. Even after deciding on the 23 players who would be taken to the competition, he was still aware of the problems he would have to face. His fears were not so much about the core team but more about the second string players.

«Portuguese football is killing the future of the Portuguese team,» Luiz Felipe told me many times.

«Clubs do what they're supposed to: they look for good players, not caring about their nationalities, but with scarcely more than 40% of Portuguese players playing in the League, what can a manager do?» he questioned.

Four years in a row, Scolari and his team had been looking for alternatives in specific positions, on the left side of defence, for instance.

«Since Rui Jorge and Nuno Valente we have never had a true left-sided player. And there are no alternatives, I mean, I have looked under the same rocks,» Murtosa joked.

But for Scolari, his biggest problem was the midfield. He felt that a fragile left wing would be compensated by Paulo Ferreira's commitment and the spirit of Ricardo Carvalho and Pepe. The criticisms he heard about the lack of strikers didn't worry him as they were the same ones he'd been hearing ever since he had arrived in Lisbon. But it was in the midfield that a game was decided. Scolari had no alternative to Deco. He had put his faith in Petit, and had hoped that Moutinho would make him forget about Maniche. He waited for Deco's big return – Deco who had been out for a few months due to an injury. He prayed that 'The Magician' would recover as he had no one else to put in his place.

The alternatives were all 'conservative': Fernando Meira is a centre midfielder who can adapt to being an attacking midfielder; Raul Meireles is a good option but he is not a creative player; Miguel Veloso can be lots of things but he just doesn't make enough of the opportunities; finally there is Jorge Ribeiro, who, to be honest, ended up being not much more than someone who gave the team a few humorous moments.

Added to all of this, Scolari had anticipated the pressure that might blow up around Cristiano Ronaldo. But he could never have imagined Cristiano's everyday life, before and after the competition, would turn into such a media circus with all the attention that the Spanish press paid him. There's no doubt in my mind that Cristiano's performance was far below what he might have achieved under different circumstances, and it didn't help the Portuguese team.

In spite of everything, Scolari believed Portugal could go far in the competition – even get to the final and win it. If the core eleven worked without any major problems then things should have gone smoothly, especially because they were players of such quality when compared to many of their opponents.

Even operating at 70% of his best, Cristiano Ronaldo is always a plus. And there were Simão, Nuno Gomes and, of course, Deco. 'The Magician', just as he had promised in Viseu, played his best Euro competition ever.

«We need to study the opponents so as to be able to impose ourselves easily,» Luiz Felipe told me on the eve of the Portugal-Turkey match. And during that game, as in the one against the Czech Republic, Portugal justified the dreams of its players. The football was very good, there was the capacity to overcome difficulties, quality both in defence and attack and a winning mindset.

What Scolari didn't plan on was Germany coming second in its group and becoming an obstacle for Portugal in the quarter-finals.

«Now or later, we will have to measure ourselves against the strongest teams in order to get to the final,» Luiz Felipe said without being able to hide his concerns.

«Germany's history of success in the final stages of the competition always weighs on the players' minds. At that moment when we try to get the ball, a moment of doubt, we'll be thinking that on the other side will be a German player and that will hurt us.»

It seems Scolari was second-guessing what ended up happening in the quarter-finals. In three apparently very similar incidents, the Portuguese players lost out to the determination of the Germans. They'd hesitated when hesitation was not a choice and, because of that, they let in three goals. The psychological disadvantage of facing up to Germany's power and tradition left Portugal showing its frailties.

«We saw the same type of moves over and over again. Everybody knew exactly what to do, which player to deal with individually, the movement, the path the ball would take. Everything was studied down to the millimetre... and everything went wrong. The players decided to change some things and there was nothing I could do. I'm not blaming them, Zé, because I've always told them to make their own decisions on the pitch but the truth is that everything went exactly the opposite to what we'd worked on. I wish I could have said goodbye differently, obviously with a victory but, more than anything else, with a display that would allow no doubts about the quality of the team. It's a huge disappointment Zé, a huge disappointment....»

MY FRIEND, THE PRESIDENT
ALMOST UNTIL THE END

During the time that Scolari was manager of the Portuguese national team, the FPF president, Gilberto Madaíl, was always a friend. They had a close relationship which was really only shaken by the Dragutinovic incident.

Unlike some football commentators in Portugal, I consider Madaíl to be a serious and committed man, who has transformed the face of the FPF over the twelve years that he's been in charge. When he first started, in May 1996, economist Gilberto Madaíl found a Federation that was failing financially and close to bankruptcy. In contrast, in June 2008, the FPF was making 3.5 million Euros per year, had traded its old building in Praça da Alegria for a modern one in Alexandre Herculano Street and had a healthy bank balance. Portugal's consecutive appearances in both Euro and World Cup competitions had resulted in considerable prize monies being received from UEFA and FIFA.

Under Madaíl's leadership, the FPF became an equal partner with some of the biggest federations in the world, gaining a position and a status in those areas of football where the decisions are made, as well as establishing a worthy reputation.

Madaíl likes to be close to the team manager and he has learned, over time, what he can and can't do publicly regarding their work. Over a 12 year period, he has had to choose four new managers (not counting the process initiated by the departure of Scolari) and his choices have often been surprising.

During Euro 96, which was held in England, he was surprised by António Oliveira's decision to swap the Portugal team for FC

Porto. He opted, then, for one of the most renowned Portuguese managers, Artur Jorge, who, nevertheless, had an unfortunate campaign and failed to qualify Portugal for the World Cup in France.

To replace Artur Jorge, he chose, against all odds, Humberto Coelho, who had been away from football for years, but whose results ended up being brilliant. But at the end of Euro 2000, Coelho decided to leave stating that Madaíl had not done enough to sort out the contract renewal in time.

In July 2000, Madaíl had two options: Carlos Queiroz and António Oliveira. Although he was advised to go with the former, he chose the latter which time proved to be a bad choice. Portugal qualified easily for the 2002 World Cup but after that Oliveira's attitude towards everybody in the FPF changed radically. A tension built up which ran through to the last day of the competition in South Korea. A few months before the World Cup, Madaíl almost fired Oliveira but ended up renewing his contract for another two years. In the end though he dismissed him, and as a result was forced to pay Oliveira compensation.

Choosing Luiz Felipe Scolari was also a surprise but also one of his best decisions as FPF president. His honesty, his working methods, his daily presence in his office (unlike Oliveira), the link he established with the players – all these things helped to build the bond between manager and President. They supported and defended each other publicly whenever they could, answering the critics and their attacks in perfect synchronism, in a way that helped the team to grow stronger.

The first test happened days before Euro 2004 when Scolari had to publicly refuse Benfica's invitation. Madaíl knew about the club's approach whilst at the same time Scolari knew the president was waiting for Portugal's results in the competition before offering him a contract renewal. When, during the press conference in Alvalade, after the match against Holland, Scolari announced that he would 'remarry' Madaíl – making the famous gesture of putting the ring on his finger – their relationship became much more than one of just employer and employee, it moved to a personal level, a level of friendship.

During the following years nothing significant happened until the period of high tension which they both lived through during the 2006 World Cup. As I've said earlier, by the time Portugal played Germany in the competition, Madaíl was not sure he could keep Scolari and it wasn't only because the manager's family didn't want to return to Brazil. The first sign of distancing between them happened during the period when it was decided that the new contract would end in 2008 and not in 2010 as Scolari had requested.

But the worst moment was, undoubtedly, the Dragutinovic incident. Although he didn't admit it at the time, Madaíl really considered dismissing Scolari, (he said so later), and the only reason that he hesitated was the lack of a better alternative and the risk that it could have for the team. Nevertheless, when the FPF decided to punish Luiz Felipe with a 35,000 Euro fine, Scolari saw the gesture as a public act of condemnation and a lack of solidarity not so much because of the amount itself but because the fine was three times more than those that UEFA usually applied.

I know that that was the turning point for Scolari, the moment that he realised that, regardless of Portugal's results in Euro 2008, he would not extend the contract beyond 30 June 2008.

Madaíl and Scolari grew apart because of small things, such as the President's absence from some of the matches, for example the Portugal-Greece game, in Dusseldorf. It was here that the business of the bonus payments became an issue with two of the players. Scolari was left to deal with it by himself even though it was something with which he shouldn't have been involved. In Madaíl's absence, Luiz Felipe called the vice-president, Amândio de Carvalho, and threw open the exit doors for the discontented players.

There were times when bonus payments had been a reason of joy. In 2004, before the Euro, Scolari had thought that he could introduce to the team the same system he had previously operated with the Brazilian team: instead of using a percentage scheme to divide the money amongst the players, managers and the rest of the staff, he proposed dividing the fund into equal parts and giving everybody the same share.

In a diplomatic way, he managed to get Luís Figo to present the idea to the team and it was accepted, without objection. The system was maintained in 2006 and 2008 but once Figo had gone, certain voices began to talk about it even though previously they had said yes and never commented on it. This was one of the reasons that led Scolari to believe that things were never going to be the same again. His decision to nominate five captains was a confirmation that he didn't believe there was a true leader of the group.

When the players gathered in Viseu, in a pre-competition training period, Madaíl already knew that Scolari was leaving after Euro 2008. But both men agreed to maintain the sense of planning for the future in public so as to give the team stability. It was an unhappy decision as everybody in the team knew that Luiz Felipe was leaving. They didn't know where he was going, but the news about the Chelsea approach had been all over the press for over a month. Still, on June 11, when Chelsea decided to announce the name of their new manager on their internet site both Scolari and Madaíl were taken by surprise. The president had been informed by the manager that he had reached an agreement with his new club but he was convinced – like Scolari

– that Abramovich would wait until the end of Euro 2008 before announcing it. In my opinion, what happened was a pure and simple demonstration of the power of money. Abramovich's Chelsea were polite enough to inform Scolari that they were announcing his name that very same night. And as soon as Scolari knew, he informed Madaíl. Both agreed that there was nothing they could do to control the situation.

Despite everything, Scolari and Madaíl had, until the end, a relationship that was based on respect and mutual support.

*The only thing
that is going to
change is the country
I'm going to live in.*

PORTUGAL WILL MISS HIM
A POWERFUL INHERITANCE

The Euro 2008 qualification period ended up bringing far more problems and controversies than Scolari had expected. After the Germany World Cup, the team could no longer count on Figo and Pauleta, two key players both on and off the pitch. Scolari's challenge was to take a young team and get it to achieve at the same level of performance as the previous one had. Cristiano Ronaldo, Simão, Nuno Gomes and Costinha would be the most important players in this strategy. But soon the problems began, some the result of injuries and others, as I've said in this book, the result of the manager feeling that the trust that he had placed in some of the players had not been reciprocated.

Losing to Poland and drawing with Serbia, in Alvalade, plus all that happened next, were critical moments. But the truth is that at the most critical moments, the players did rise to the occasion and responded to their manager and to the expectations of a demanding public. In the end, when you look at the maths, Portugal did actually get more points than Scolari had initially expected and they qualified for Euro 2008. But that wasn't enough for Scolari's critics.

When the competition ended, Scolari's link to the Portugal team ended too. This is a normal situation for any manager – many believe that being more than three or four years in the same place is not good for either manager or players. They can lose the ability to motivate, surprise and improve. The worst that can happen to a football team is routine, with all the negative things that that can imply.

Luiz Felipe Scolari leaves Portugal a unique legacy: more games, more wins, more goals scored and three consecutive qualifications in major competitions.

He's no angel, but neither is he a demon. For more than 20 years I had the privilege to follow the Portuguese team closely, to meet its managers, some in a more personal way, others just through the work. During my four year period as the FPF press officer I worked with Humberto Coelho, António Oliveira, Agostinho Oliveira and Luiz Felipe Scolari. The first two I'd already known since they'd been players and so it was not difficult for me to deal with them in the work environment.

Agostinho Oliveira, although he only had a brief period as a manager, was always a gentleman.

Scolari, I only met properly on 15 December 2002, the day he was presented as the team's new leader – though two weeks earlier on, on December 1, I met him briefly and shook his hand at the 2002 World Cup draw in Pusang. We worked together until 30 April 2003, in other words a little more than four months.

Over the following five years, our relationship has grown and become stronger. And at the end of those five years, I have no doubts when I say that the Portuguese team will miss Scolari.

And even his severest critics will too.

AN UNPARALLELED CAREER

Luiz Felipe Scolari was born 9 November 1948 in Passo Fundo, in Rio Grande do Sul, the southern-most region of Brazil. Married to Olga Pasinato, he has two sons: Leonardo and Fabrizio. As a player, his career didn't get very far. He was a central defender who started playing at the age of 17, in the Aimoré's youth league. Later he moved to Caxias, Novo Hamburgo, Juventude and CSA. It was in the latter club that he started his managerial career, which continued as follows: Juventude, Brasil de Pelotas, Al-Shabab (Saudi Arabia), Pelotas, Juventude (for the second time), Grémio, Goiás, Al Qadisiya (Kuwait), Kuwait's National team, Curitiba, Criciúma, Al Ahli (Saudi Arabia), Al Qadisiya (for the second time), Grémio (for the second time), Jubilo Iwata (Japan), Palmeiras, Cruzeiro, Brazilian national team, Portuguese national team. He is currently manager of Chelsea FC.

SCOLARI'S CLUBS

As a Player

1973–1979	Caxias
1980	Juventude
1980–1981	Novo Hamburgo
1981	Centro Sportivo Alagoano

As Manager

1982	Centro Sportivo Alagoano
1982–1983	Juventude
1983	Brasil de Pelotas
1984–1985	Al-Shabab
1986	Brasil de Pelotas
1986–1987	Juventude
1987	Grêmio
1988	Goiás
1988–1990	Al Qadisiya
1990	Kuwait
1991	Criciúma
1991	Al-Ahli
1992	Al Qadisiya
1993–1996	Grêmio
1997	Júbilo Iwata
1997–2000	Palmeiras
2000–2001	Cruzeiro
2001–2002	Brazil
2003–2008	Portugal
2008–	Chelsea F.C.

MANAGERIAL ACHIEVEMENTS

1987	Gaúcho Champions (Grêmio)
1990	Kuwait Cup (Al Qadisiya)
	Gulf Cup (Al Qadisiya)
1991	Brazil Cup (Criciúma)
1994	Brazil Cup (Grêmio)
1995	South American Club Champions (Grêmio)
	Libertadores da América Cup (Grêmio)
	Gaúcho Champions (Grémio)
1996	Brazilian League Champions (Grêmio)
	Gaúcho Champions (Grêmio)
	South American Cup (Grêmio)
1997	Runners up Brazilian League (Palmeiras)
1998	Brazil Cup (Palmeiras)
	Mercosur Cup (Palmeiras)
1999	South American club champions
	– Libertadores da América Cup (Palmeiras)
	Best manager in South America
2000	South American club vice-champions (Palmeiras)
	Second runner up in the Libertadores da América Cup (Palmeiras)
	Rio-São Paulo Tournament (Palmeiras)
2001	Sul-Minas Cup (Cruzeiro)
2002	1st place in the World Cup (Brazil)
	Best manager in the world (IFHHS)
	Best manager in South America
2004	Runners up Euro 2004 (Portugal)
2006	4th place in the World Cup (Portugal)
2008	Euro 2008 quarter-finals (Portugal)

PORTUGAL'S MATCH RECORD

01	12-02-03	Italy	Genoa	0-1	Friendly
02	29-03-03	Brazil	Porto	2-1	Friendly
03	02-04-03	Macedonia	Lausanne	1-0	Friendly
04	30-04-03	Holland	Eindhoven	1-1	Friendly
05	06-06-03	Macedonia	Braga	0-0	Friendly
06	10-06-03	Bolivia	Lisbon	4-0	Friendly
07	20-08-03	Kazakhstan	Chaves	1-0	Friendly
08	20-08-03	Spain	Guimarães	0-3	Friendly
09	10-09-03	Norway	Oslo	1-0	Friendly
10	11-10-03	Albania	Lisbon	5-3	Friendly
11	15-11-03	Greece	Aveiro	1-1	Friendly
12	19-11-03	Kuwait	Leiria	8-0	Friendly
13	19-02-04	England	Faro/Loulé	1-1	Friendly
14	31-03-04	Italy	Braga	1-2	Friendly
15	28-04-04	Sweden	Coimbra	2-2	Friendly
16	29-05-04	Luxembourg	Águeda	3-0	Friendly
17	05-06-04	Lithuania	Setúbal	4-1	Friendly
18	12-06-04	Greece	Porto	1-2	Euro 2004
19	16-06-04	Russia	Lisbon	2-0	Euro 2004
20	20-06-04	Spain	Lisbon	1-0	Euro 2004
21	24-06-04	England	Lisbon	2-2[1]	Euro 2004
22	30-06-04	Holland	Lisbon	2-1	Euro 2004
23	04-07-04	Greece	Lisbon	0-1	Final Euro 2004
24	04-09-04	Latvia	Riga	2-0	Qual. World Cup 06
25	08-09-04	Estonia	Leiria	4-0	Qual. World Cup 06
26	09-10-04	Liechtenstein	Vaduz	2-2	Qual. World Cup 06
27	13-10-04	Russia	Lisbon	7-1	Qual. World Cup 06
28	17-11-04	Luxembourg	Luxembourg	5-0	Qual. World Cup 06
29	09-02-05	Rep. Ireland	Dublin	0-1	Friendly
30	26-03-05	Canada	Barcelos	4-1	Friendly

31	30-03-05	Slovakia	Bratislava	1-1	Qual. World Cup 06
32	04-06-05	Slovakia	Lisbon	2-0	Qual. World Cup 06
33	08-06-05	Estonia	Tallinn	1-0	Qual. World Cup 06
34	17-08-05	Egypt	Ponta Delgada	2-0	Friendly
35	03-09-05	Luxembourg	Faro/Loulé	6-0	Qual. World Cup 06
36	07-09-05	Russia	Moscow	0-0	Qual. World Cup 06
37	08-10-05	Liechtenstein	Aveiro	2-1	Qual. World Cup 06
38	12-10-05	Latvia	Porto	3-0	Qual. World Cup 06
39	12-11-05	Croatia	Coimbra	2-0	Friendly
40	15-11-05	N. Ireland	Belfast	1-1	Friendly
41	01-03-06	Saudi Arabia	Dusseldorf	3-0	Friendly
42	27-05-06	Cape Verde	Évora	4-1	Friendly
43	03-06-06	Luxembourg	Metz	3-0	Friendly
44	11-06-06	Angola	Cologne	1-0	World Cup'06
45	17-06-06	Iran	Frankfurt	2-0	World Cup'06
46	21-06-06	Mexico	Gelsenkirchen	2-1	World Cup'06
47	25-06-06	Holland	Nuremberg	1-0	World Cup'06
48	01-07-06	England	Gelsenkirch.[2]	0-0	World Cup'06
49	05-07-06	France	Munich	0-1	World Cup'06
50	01-09-06	Germany	Stuttgart	1-3	3/4 World Cup'06
51	01-09-06	Denmark	Brondby	2-4	Friendly
52	06-09-06	Finland	Helsinki	1-1	Qual. Euro 2008
53	07-10-06	Azerbaijan	Porto	3-0	Qual. Euro 2008
54	11-10-06	Poland	Chorzów	1-2	Qual. Euro 2008
55	15-11-06	Kazakhstan	Coimbra	3-0	Qual. Euro 2008
56	06-02-07	Brazil	London	2-0	Friendly
57	24-03-07	Belgium	Lisbon	4-0	Qual. Euro 2008
58	28-03-07	Serbia	Belgrade	1-1	Qual. Euro 2008
59	02-06-07	Belgium	Brussels	2-1	Qual. Euro 2008
60	05-06-07	Kuwait	Kuwait	1-1	Friendly

PORTUGAL'S MATCH RECORD

61	22-08-07	Armenia	Erevan	1-1	Qual. Euro 2008
62	08-09-07	Poland	Lisbon	2-2	Qual. Euro 2008
63	12-09-07	Serbia	Lisbon	1-1	Qual. Euro 2008
64	13-10-07	Azerbaijan	Baku	2-0	Qual. Euro 2008
65	17-10-07	Kazakhstan	Almaty	2-1	Qual. Euro 2008
66	17-11-07	Armenia	Leiria	1-0	Qual. Euro 2008
67	21-11-07	Finland	Porto	0-0	Qual. Euro 2008
68	06-02-08	Italy	Zurich	1-3	Friendly
69	26-03-08	Greece	Düsseldorf	1-3	Friendly
70	31-05-08	Georgia	Viseu	2-0	Friendly
71	07-06-08	Turkey	Geneva	2-0	Euro 2008
72	11-06-08	Czech Rep.	Geneva	3-1	Euro 2008
73	15-06-08	Switzerland	Basel	0-2	Euro 2008
74	19-06-08	Germany	Basel	2-3	Euro 2008

(1) 5-4 penalty kicks (against England)

(2) 3-1 penalty kicks (against England)

SUMMARY

	Official	Friendly	Total
Games	43	31	74
Wins	24	17	41
Draws	12	7	19
Defeats	7	7	14
Goals Scored	82	63	145
Goals Against	33	30	63

PORTUGAL'S OTHER MANAGERS

	Games	Wins	Defeats	Draws	For	Against
Luiz Felipe Scolari	74	41	19	14	145	63
António Oliveira	44	26	10	8	102	40
Júlio Cernadas Pereira	39	16	9	14	52	51
José Maria Antunes	31	9	4	18	40	59
Cândido de Oliveira	31	8	9	14	51	61
Tavares da Silva	29	10	4	15	46	61
Humberto Coelho	24	16	4	4	56	16
Carlos Queiróz	23	10	8	5	28	14
Artur Jorge	20	9	8	3	24	11
José Torres	17	8	1	8	21	23
José Maria Pedroto	17	7	4	6	15	2
José Augusto	15	9	4	2	29	12
José Gomes da Silva	13	5	4	4	17	13
Salvador do Carmo	13	3	4	6	17	35
Mário Wilson	10	5	2	3	12	12

The positions and people mentioned in this summary relate to the period covered in the book

Afonso de Melo (Portugal Team Press Officer)
Agostinho Oliveira (FPF manager)
Alex Ferguson, Sir (Manchester United Manager)
Amândio de Carvalho (Vice-President of the FPF)
Ana Matias (Sports Marketeer)
André (FC Porto Assistant Manager)
Angel Sanchez (Referee)
Antero Henrique (FC Porto Board member)
António Gonçalves (Portugal Team kit manager)
António Magalhães (*Record* reporter)
António Oliveira (FPF manager)
Ariza Makukula (Marítimo player)
Avram Grant (Chelsea Manager, 2007/2008)
Benny McCarthy (FC Porto player)
Bernando Ribeiro (*Record* reporter)
Brian Barwick (FA Chief Executive)
Bruno Vale (FC Porto player)
Cafú (Brazilian team player)
Carlos Godinho (FPF manager)
Carlos Martins (Sporting and Recreativo Huelva player)
Carlos Queiróz (Portugal Manager, 1991-93 & from July 2008)
Céu Freitas (*Record* reporter)
Co Adriaanse (FC Porto Manager)
Costinha (FC Porto and Dynamo Moscow player)
Cristiano Ronaldo (Manchester United player)
Darius Vassel (England player)
Darlan Schneider (Portugal fitness coach)

David James (England player)
Deco (FC Porto and Portugal player)
Émerson (Brazilian team player)
Fabrizio Scolari (Scolari's son)
Fernando Brassard (Portugal goalkeeping coach)
Fernando Couto (Lazio player)
Fernando Henrique Cardoso (President of Brazil)
Flávio Teixeira 'Murtosa' (Portugal team coach)
Florentino Pérez (President of Real Madrid)
Frederico Fellini (Filmmaker)
Gilberto Madaíl (President of the FPF)
Gilmar Veloz (Football agent)
Harry Been (General-secretary of the Dutch FA)
Hélder Postiga (Tottenham and FC Porto player)
Howard Wilkinson (former England Manager)
Hugo Almeida (Werder Bremen player)
Humberto Coelho (former Portugal Manager)
Ivete Sangalo (Singer)
Ivica Dragutinovic (Serbian team player)
João Roberto Gretz (Brazilian public speaker and writer)
João Rodrigues (former FPF President)
João Pinto (Sporting Lisbon player)
Joaquim Oliveira (Businessman)
Jorge Andrade (Deportivo La Coruna player)
Jorge Mendes (Football agent)
José António Camacho (Manager of Benfica)
José Coelho (Sculptor)
José Couceiro (Vitória de Setúbal player)
José Eduardo Bettencourt (Chief Executive, Sporting Lisbon)
José Eduardo Moniz (Chief Executive, TVI)
José Manuel Freitas (*A Bola* reporter)
José Maria Carvalho (Olival's Training Centre manager)

José Maria Pedroto (former FC Porto Manager)

José Mourinho (FC Porto Manager 2002-4, Chelsea, Inter Milan)

José Peseiro (Sporting Lisbon Manager)

José Veiga (Football agent)

Khalid Boulahrouz (Dutch team player)

Leida (Scolari's mother)

Leonardo Scolari (Scolari's son)

Lisete Teixeira (Flávio Teixeira's wife)

Luís Aragonês (Manager of Spain)

Luís Filipe Vieira (President of Benfica)

Luís Figo (Real Madrid and Inter Milan player)

Luís Sousa (*O Jogo* reporter)

Maniche (FC Porto and Dynamo Moscow player)

Manolo Vidal (Director of Football at Sporting Lisbon)

Manuel José (Manager of Al-Ahli)

Marcelo Lippi (Manager of Italy)

Marco Caneira (Sporting Lisbon and Valencia player)

Miguel (Benfica and Valencia player)

Miguel Pedro Vieira (*Record* reporter)

Miguel Ribeiro Telles (President of Sporting Lisbon)

Miguel Veloso (Sporting Lisbon player)

Nélson (Sporting Lisbon player)

Nuno Gomes (Benfica player)

Nuno Valente (FC Porto and Everton player)

Otto Rehhagel (Manager of Greece)

Panenka (former Czechoslovakia player)

Paul Mony Samuel (FIFA delegate)

Pauleta (Paris Saint-Germain player)

Paulo Bento (Sporting Lisbon Manager)

Paulo Calado (*Record* photographer)

Paulo Ferreira (FC Porto and Chelsea player)

Paulo Santos (Sporting Braga player)

Pedro Mil-Homens (Manager of Academia Sporting)
Pepe (Real Madrid player)
Peter Kenyon (Chief Executive, Chelsea FC)
Pinto da Costa (President of FC Porto)
Quim (Sporting Braga and Benfica player)
Regina Brandão (Sports psychologist)
Ricardo (Boavista, Sporting Lisbon and Real Bétis player)
Ricardo Carvalho (FC Porto and Chelsea player)
Ricardo Quaresma (FC Porto player)
Ricardo Rocha (Benfica player)
Ricardo Teixeira (President of the CBF, Brazil)
Rivaldo (Brazilian team player)
Roberto Carlos (Brazilian team player)
Roberto Leal (Singer)
Roman Abramovich (Owner of Chelsea FC)
Romário (Brazilian team player)
Ronaldo (Brazilian team player)
Rui Barros (FC Porto coach)
Rui Caçador (FPF manager)
Ruy Carlos Ostermann (Journalist)
Saddam Hussein (Former President of Iraq)
Samuel Pedroso (FPF's audiovisual technician)
Sebastião Lazaroni (Manager of Marítimo)
Sérgio Conceição (Lazio player)
Simão Sabrosa (Benfica and Atlético Madrid player)
Sun Tzu (Chinese military strategist)
Sven-Göran Eriksson (Former England Manager)
Tiago (Benfica, Chelsea and Lyon player)
Tonel (Sporting Lisbon player)
Valentin Ivanov (Referee)
Viecheslav Koloskov (President of Russian Football Federation)
Vítor Baía (FC Porto player)

BIBLIOGRAPHIC SOURCES

Scolari, A Alma do Penta,
(Ruy C. Osterman, Booktree, 2003)
Deco, O Preço da Glória,
(Sérgio Alves, Prime Books, 2003)
Ricardo, Diário de um Sonho,
(Luís M. Pereira, Prime Books, 2004)
Pauleta, O Ciclone dos Açores,
(José M. Freitas, Prime Books, 2004)
Cristiano Ronaldo, Momentos,
(Manuel Brandão, Ideias e Rumos, 2007)

Record
A Bola
Jornada
A Folha de S.Paulo
O Globo
The Sun
The Daily Mail
Wikipédia

Other titles from
Dewi Lewis Media

For full details of all our titles
please visit our website at

www.dewilewismedia.com

RAFA BENÍTEZ

the authorised biography
by Paco Lloret

£12.99 softback, 224 pages
ISBN: 978-0-954684-37-2

In this authorised biography, Paco Lloret gives real insight into what motivates Rafa Benítez, his attention to detail, his man-mangement skills, his sharp football mind and his constant quest to develop the skills of himself and his players. We discover the steely determination with which he faced his early setbacks, his personal trauma at the tragic death of his brother-in-law, his public anger after the Madrid bombings, and the complex intrigue at Valencia which led to his move to Liverpool.

JOSÉ MOURINHO
MADE IN PORTUGAL

the authorised biography
by Luís Lourenço

£12.99 softback, 224 pages
ISBN: 978-0-954684-33-4

When José Mourinho arrived in London in 2004 he had an immediate and frequently controversial impact on English football. This fascinating book charts his rise from relatively humble beginnings as assistant coach to Bobby Robson, to become the most sought-after club manager in Europe. Long-term friend, Portuguese journalist Luís Lourenço guides us through the formative years, as Mourinho returns to Portugal from Barcelona at the turn of the millennium to embark on the remarkable journey which led him to Chelsea.

JAMES LAWTON
ON FOOTBALL

introduced by John Giles

£9.99 softback, 256 pages
ISBN: 978-1-905928-02-6

All human emotion is there. James's words educate, inspire and seduce. He is a master craftsman.' – James Nesbitt, actor

On Football brings together a selection of the best from the columns of James Lawton. His writing gives a powerful commentary on the state of football over the last decade. Lawton never pulls his punches, writing with both intelligence and wit, and with an enviable knowledge and understanding of the game.

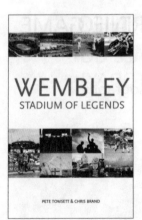

WEMBLEY
STADIUM OF LEGENDS

Pete Tomsett & Chris Brand

£12.99 hardback, 160 pages
ISBN: 978-0-954684-39-6

Wembley: Stadium Of Legends combines remarkable archive images with fascinating information: tales of enigmatic entrepreneurs and entertainers, courageous athletes and odds-defying sportsmen. Through unique photographs, the later chapters tell of the transition from old to new, from the faded grandeur of the old stadium, through its demolition, especially the heartbreaking destruction of the twin towers, to the construction of the new building and its dramatic arch.

ON CRICKET

by James Lawton

introduced by Michael Atherton
edited by Ivan Ponting

£9.99 softback, 256 pages
ISBN: 978-1-905928-04-0

In a career which has included coverage of Test cricket at home and abroad James Lawton, Chief Sports Writer at *The Independent* has had the opportunity to observe and know such legends as Botham, Lara, Warne, McGrath, Tendulkar, and Ponting. Currently *Sports Writer of the Year*, his trenchant opinions on cricket, and life, have led his column to be amongst the most admired and celebrated of the last decade.

PRAWNS IN THE GAME
HOW FOOTBALL GOT WHERE IT IS TODAY!

Paul French

£9.99 softback, 224 pages
ISBN: 978-0-954684-38-9

Something grotesque is going on in the beautiful game. Money rather than sport now rules the roost. Stadium names are sold off to the highest bidder and players often seem no more than overpaid and over-sexed celebrities. Their every action, both on and off the pitch, is fodder for the tabloids as the players themselves argue over whether it's £100k or £120k a week in their pay packets. Written by a fan for the fans, you'll laugh, you'll get angry and you'll find out: how did the prawn sandwich brigade take over the national sport?

THE ROAD FROM WIGAN PIER

Wigan Athletic's rise from
non-league to Premier League

by Andrew Ross
foreword Dave Whelan & Paul Jewell

£9.99 softback, 224 pages
ISBN: 978-1-905928-01-9

In ten short years Wigan Athletic have gone from the bottom of the Football League and the verge of bankruptcy, to millionaires' row, proudly sitting alongside the Chelseas and Manchester Uniteds of this world. How they got there is extraordinary. This is not just a story of a small town football club struggling for years before rescue by a local multimillionaire. It is a story of dreams and disasters, of faltering attempts to establish a foothold for the game in the town – to finally emerge triumphant at the pinnacle of English football.

ALAIN BAXTER
UNFINISHED BUSINESS

the authorised biography
by Andrew Ross

£12.99 softback, 224 pages
ISBN: 978-0-954684-35-8

Nicknamed 'The Highlander', Baxter first skied aged 2. By his teens he dreamt of challenging for top honours. He began a ten year slog, driving around Europe, living on overdraft, sleeping in hostels or in his car. In 2002 Baxter caused the biggest Winter Olympic upset by clinching Britain's first ever skiing medal. Agonisingly, the ecstasy was short-lived. After a hero's welcome home he learned that he had failed a drugs test and would be stripped of his medal. Stunned and mystified Baxter began the challenge which would eventually clear his name.